DEAD RECKONINGS

A Review of Horror and the Weird in the Arts
Edited by Alex Houstoun and Michael J. Abolafia

No. 25 (Spring 2019)

3   A Look Behind "The Challenge from Beyond"....................
Michael D. Miller

12   Finding the Everything in Nothing......... Christopher Ropes
Simon Strantzas, *Nothing Is Everything.*

16   Weird Fiction and Decadence ....S. T. Joshi
James Machin, *Weird Fiction in Britain 1880–1939.*

22   That Is Not How the Story Goes .... Bev Vincent
Theodora Goss, *Snow White Learns Witchcraft: Stories and Poems.*

25   Sesqua Valley's Weirdest Inhabitant, Wilum Pugmire ....
David Barker

28   Ramsey's Rant: Horror versus Horror......Ramsey Campbell

33   Marvelous Milicent: The Rise and Removal of a
Monster-Artist Maven .... Danel Olson
Mallory O'Meara, *The Lady from the Black Lagoon: Hollywood
Monsters and the Lost Legacy of Milicent Patrick.*

38   Maybe Johnny is an Old One? *The Room* as Lovecraftian
Pastiche.. Edward Guimont

49   Weird Fiction in the 21st Century: A Conversation with
S. T. Joshi... Alex Houstoun

62   Rediscovering Ken Greenhall .... Darrell Schweitzer
Ken Greenhall, *Elizabeth; Hell Hound;* and *Childgrave.*

66   Some Notes on *Call of Cthulhu* and Other Lovecraftian
Video Games ....Géza A. G. Reilly
Call of Cthulhu: The Official Video Game.

70   Running Towards Nothing: B. Catling's Vorrh Trilogy......
Daniel Pietersen
B. Catling, *The Vorrh; The Erstwhile;* and *The Cloven.*

75 The Horror of Mendacity .... Acep Hale
   Daniel Powell, *Horror Culture in the New Millennium: Digital Dissonance and Technohorror.*

80 Marvelous Monsters..Hank Wagner
   Anya Martin, *Sleeping with the Monster.*

82 Men Kill Women Like Me....................... Fiona Maeve Geist
   Farah Rose Smith, *Anonyma.*

86 Meditations on the Agnostic Gothic ... Karen Joan Kohoutek

95 About the Contributors

DEAD RECKONINGS is published by Hippocampus Press, P.O. Box 641, New York, NY 10156 (www.hippocampuspress.com). Copyright © 2019 by Hippocampus Press. Cover art by Jason C. Eckhardt. Cover design by Barbara Briggs Silbert. Hippocampus Press logo by Anastasia Damianakos. Orders and subscriptions should be sent to Hippocampus Press. Contact Alex Houstoun at deadreckoningsjournal@gmail.com for assignments or before submitting a publication for review.

ISSN 1935-6110
ISBN 978-1-61498-272-2

A Look Behind "The Challenge from Beyond"

Michael D. Miller

Among the few stories fans and scholars of H. P. Lovecraft often overlook or dismiss is the seminal composite or "round-robin" weird tale "The Challenge from Beyond," published in *Fantasy Magazine* for September 1935. In hindsight, there are a few considerations that should make this tale much more significant than it is, as "The Challenge" fits uniquely in the annals of Lovecraft's work. The story is not an individual composition nor a collaboration nor a "work-for-hire" ghost-writing assignment. More importantly, the two major contributors, Howard and Lovecraft, were still in the midst of an almost six-year argument over the value of civilization during the composition of the story. By analyzing their personal letters on the subject, we begin to see much of the subtext behind their individual contributions to "The Challenge."

The inspiration for the round-robin came from *Fantasy Magazine* editor Julius Schwartz (of the All-American Publications, later DC Comics fame), who proposed two versions of the story: one for the weird fiction field and the other for the emerging science fiction market. This idea was specifically to celebrate the third anniversary of *Fantasy Magazine,* but these composite tales were also marketing gimmicks to boost sales. The log line on the cover to the issue boasted: "10 Authors— All Stars." Lovecraft, C. L. Moore, A. Merritt, Robert E. Howard, and Frank Belknap Long were contracted for the weird version; Stanley G. Weinbaum, Donald Wandrei, E. E. "Doc" Smith, Harl Vincent, and Murray Leinster would compose the speculative version. The stature of these pulp-era luminaries set the expectations high, but their results seem to have left us with little merit (most especially with the later science fiction version by Weinbaum et al.).

There is ample reason to preemptively dismiss these round-robin creations, as stories of this type often fall short of expectations due, perhaps, to the fragility of holding narrative stability between several authors (something deconstructionists might appreciate), or the use of composite composition as a standard "creative writing" exercise for student writers. Lovecraft has noted his own dissatisfaction of the process:

> About that composite story—my section does not include it. It is a five-author affair, in the following order: [C. L.] Moore, [Abraham] Merritt, HPL, Two-Gun Bob [Howard], Frank B. Long. My section was perhaps the most difficult, since I had to plan out the general rationale and plot of the whole thing. All that Miss Moore and Abie did was to sketch out the background and plaster on atmosphere. There was no story up to the point where I was expected to begin, and at that stage (the third instalment out of five—i.e. the central section) it was imperative that somebody start something and give an idea of what it was all about. I fear I made a mess of it. The assignment reached me just as I was leaving St. Augustine, and I did the job in odd moments of Charleston sightseeing. There was no chance for original creation, so I fell very reprehensibly into a hackneyed pattern. I surely hope that no one will judge me by this attempt! (*Selected Letters* 5.199)

While Lovecraft might be unduly, but characteristically, harsh on his section, his overall judgment of the process is quite accurate.

The story opens with Moore's initiative, establishing the character—George Campbell, a professor of geology (a perhaps standard Lovecraftian character-type)—a setting, some remote Canadian woodland where Campbell is on vacation, and the first plot-point: Campbell's discovery of a strange crystal cube among some rocks outside his tent—all in two and a half pages. Of note is one specific description she gives to the crystal: "For embedded in its center lay a little disc of a pale and nameless substance with characters incised deep upon its quartz-enclosed surface. Wedge-shaped characters faintly reminiscent of cuneiform writing" (504). We then shift to Merritt, who produces a less-than-stellar plot advancement in two pages. Merritt was the best-known writer of the group, but all he gives us is that Campbell becomes fixated on the crystal and through his meddling activates the power-disc in-

side and is teleported into it. This lack of effort from such a pulp luminary did not go unnoticed by Lovecraft, nor the ease of being the second writer out of five in the composite process. From the same letter:

> Amusingly enough, Abe Merritt very boldly dodged the hard job of a central assignment. [Julius] Schwartz had originally given Long the second part to do, and Belknap had prepared a rather clever development. That put Merritt third—where he would have had to build on Long's section. Well—when it came to that, he squirmed out in what both Long and I (and Wandrei and others as well) think was a distinctly unsportsmanlike way. Claiming that Long had veered away from the subject-matter specified in the title, he refused to play unless Schwartz would kill Belknap's section and give him second place! That would of course give him a "snap" assignment—with no difficult threads to pick up, and no responsibility in developing the plot. Schwartz gave in and let him have his way—but I'll be damned if I'd have done so, despite his prominence . . . Abie demanded that the rules be arbitrarily changed in his favour! Well—he got away with it—and as a result the third and most difficult section was wished on me! (*Selected Letters* 5.199–200)

The result proved to be the best of the five contributions to the story. (Sorry, Howardians.)

If there is any doubt of Lovecraft's professional ability over his peers, one need only read this story and compare his section to the others. (I'll note that Howard's is a close second; the other writers do not come close to comparison.) In addition to his signature stylistic prose responsible for much of the mood and tone of "The Challenge"—especially in his hypnotic description of space-time-continuum travel—Lovecraft provides most of the elements of fiction in background, plotting, and the entire *raison d'être* of the story. More importantly for fans of Lovecraftian lore are the additions to his cycle of anti-myth ("Cthulhu Mythos"). We are introduced to a new, and hostile, alien race in the Yekubians, and Lovecraft adds another distancing device: a translation of the Eltdown Shards by one Arthur Brooke Winters-Hall.

The burden of making the weird, or in this case the crystal, work so that we can dispel our disbelief was no less treated in full measure by Lovecraft. This is also significant if we read Lovecraft's later stories at the height of his cosmic horror vision as proto-science-fiction tales. Precise plotting in Lovecraft's contribution is the blueprint that holds the entirety of "The Challenge from Beyond" together. Lovecraft prefaced his contribution with two pages of notes giving us the origin and civilization of the Yekubians, their creation of the power-discs enclosed in crystal to enable them to project their minds across the universe, and finally how they have used this method to subjugate, extirpate, and in some cases exterminate other life forms. The preface also contains precisely how the power-discs work—essential for the interstellar proto-science-fiction element. Lovecraft details the mechanics for mind exchange:

> . . . the mind of each being exchanged with that of a member of the mighty race. Machine [*sic*] can hold more than one mind—so that one cube on a distant planet can trap any number of beings rapidly. During the stage of complete exchange, the mind of the captured being remains in the body of its displacer—not in the wall machine—the process consisting of 2 transfers: (a) distant being to wall machine, (b) investigator exchanging with wall machine, (c) wall machine exchanging with vacant body of distant being. On several occasions planets were completely overrun and subjugated by this means—the advanced race once voluntarily remaining in its new region and bodies after the killing off of the misplaced native stock. Return accomplished in corresponding way. Extirpation accomplished by killing of distant body (quasi-suicide) at moment of return. Bodiless distant mind then returns to machine and is annihilated unless some use for it exists. ("Notes to 'The Challenge from Beyond'" 258)

This function has been pointed out as being "lifted" from "The Shadow out of Time," but Lovecraft adds the Great Race to the story as one of the life forms the Yekubians tried to possess to subvert such an assertion. Thus, this adds even further dimension to the cosmic magnitude of Lovecraft's final stories, where the human mind, our most valued resource, is unsafe in the trans-galactic gulfs of the unknown. "The Challenge" is very much a product of "The Shadow out of

Time," as it should be, given that 1935 was the final phase of Lovecraft's work. The process of mind exchange is also not unique to the Great Race but goes back to "The Thing on the Doorstep" (1933), if not before.

The most important element of "The Challenge," however, is that the story was written at the height of Howard's and Lovecraft's years long feud over "barbarism" and "civilization" (1930–36). The initial argument started when Howard indicated he had little interest in Rome or other great "civilizations," instead preferring the "northern barbarians," and Lovecraft felt a cultural need to defend civilization. The first hint of this is very clear in "The Challenge." Lovecraft's contribution—six pages, double that of the others—describes the civilization of Yekub.

> There dwelt on a world—and eventually on countless other worlds—of outer space a mighty order of worm-like beings whose attainments and whose control of natural forces surpassed anything within the range of terrestrial imagination. They had mastered the art of interstellar travel early in their career, and had peopled every habitable planet in their own galaxy—killing of the races they had found. (510)

Howard's follow-up more or less dismantles that civilization with a return to "barbarism": "He [Campbell] was drunk with the feel of power. He feared the superstitions of Yekub no more than he feared those of Earth. With that globe in his hands he would be king of Yekub. The worm men would dare deny him nothing, when he held their god as his hostage" (519).

Lovecraft's central defense of Greece and Rome (and civilization) was outlined to Howard in a letter of August 16, 1932: "They have the same general problems of the settled nations of modernity have. They had measurably conquered the salient natural phenomena around them and had won sufficient material security to expand other parts of their mental and emotional endowment than those directly connected with self-defense and ego-assertion" (*A Means to Freedom* 351). This aspect certainly could be applied to the Yekubians, and even the Yithians, in the expansion and control of galaxy after galaxy—not as a defense of these actions, but of each alien culture's eventual move to intellectual pursuits, most notably that of science. Lovecraft finishes with: "Where the barbarian had only a few simple motives and pleasures, the civilized man had the infinitely vaster variety of stimuli and rewards which accrued from a more all-around development of his capacities. What he lost in the process was far more balanced by what he gained—so that not until his later decadence did he need to mourn any of the simple ruggednesses he had left behind" (*A Means to Freedom* 351). It might have been enough to say Howard was responding to this "decadence," but his response, mostly personal and heated, was an extensive celebration of what had been "left behind." It has been noted by S. T. Joshi in his essay "Barbarism vs. Civilization" that "all the tens of thousands of words of Lovecraft's subsequent debates with Howard on this issue amount to little more than elaborations and refinements of this basic utterance" (77).

Howard's responses to this over the years are interesting, as they form the central thrust of his narrative contributions to "The Challenge from Beyond." From January 1934: "As to Barbarism and Civilization, I did not mean to intimate that more people suffer under civilization than under barbarism. I merely suggest that the barbarian does not suffer as a civilized man would suffer if forced to live under the same conditions as a barbarian" (*A Means to Freedom* 710). On the personal side, Howard writes in December 1934:

> Concerning values: there was never any real use in most of the arguments, anyway. In practically every instance the debate began the same way. I expressed a personal preference that did not coincide with yours, and you attacked me for it, apparently assuming a mere personal preference for something that you did not consider 'superior' implied a criticism of your tastes, and repudiation of 'basic values'! (808).

In February 1935, leading up to "The Challenge" assignment, Howard was quite clear in his view of civilization even quoting the support of anthropologists: "I do not believe our civilization is perfect and I reserve the right (just as you do) to criticize the phases which are objectionable." He then quotes a Professor B. Schidloff, "No thinking person who forms his own opinion on the modern times doubts any longer that civilization is equivalent to moral degeneracy" (828). This continues up through the assignment for "The Challenge"—and beyond. From December 5, 1935: "I was highly honored to be asked to contribute to 'The Challenge from Beyond' yarn, along with you, Miss Moore, Merritt and Long. I hope my share didn't weaken the strength of the story much. The rest of you did fine work, as you all always do. Appearing in such company will probably remain my chief claim to fame" (908).

The story's mid-point, written by Lovecraft, could have almost been the end of the story itself if it were a straight weird tale. Looking at his reflection on a mirror-like surface, protagonist George Campbell finds that his mind has been transplanted into the body of one of the centipede-like race of Yekubians: "Yet—horribly verifying his discolored and unfamiliar sensations—it was not his own body at all that he saw reflected in the burnished metal. It was, instead, the loathsome, pale-grey bulk of one of the great centipedes" (516). This certainly is more reminiscent of "The Outsider" (minus the Derlethian *italics*).

Howard takes over the story and, as articulated in many of his exchanges with Lovecraft, has George Campbell (in the body of a Yekubian) follow in the steps of Conan the barbarian. It is interesting to note that the inner thoughts of Campbell on his rampage to take the throne of Yekub through violence echo many of Howard's exchanges with Lovecraft. "What was his former body but a cloak, eventually to be cast off at death anyway? What had it ever given him save toil, poverty, continual frustration and repression?" "With the honesty possible only when life is stripped to its naked fundamentals, he realized that he remembered with pleasure only the physical delights of his former life" (516). As Campbell begins his rampage, "A lawless exultation rose in him. He was a man without a world, free of all conventions and inhibitions of earth, of this strange planet, free of every artificial restraint in the universe"; "Let him walk the earth slaying and destroying as he would. Earth and its races no longer had any meaning to George Campbell" (517), and so on. It does give some credence to de Camp's "a Conan among centipedes" remark (de Camp 409).

In essence, there is a nihilism in both writers and in their contributions to the story. Even Lovecraft began their debate in a letter dated January 21, 1933 by agreeing with the philosopher and historian Oswald Spengler that "all cultures must necessarily perish of old age" (*A Means to Freedom* 519). In visceral terms, for Lovecraft, the crystal is a symbol of civilization, and science, and the power to transcend the limitations of the physical universe. To Howard the crystal is a weapon, a sharp implement for gutting Yukuth, the supreme lord of science. "To Yukuth it [the crystal] was a scientific implement. He did not even know it could be used as a weapon" (518). This sums up quite well the argument behind "The Challenge from Beyond."

Howard ends his contribution with Campbell taking the throne of Yekub. Frank Belknap Long, in the last round of the composite story, takes us to the body of Campbell back on earth, now possessed by a Yekubian. Of course, only a few hours in the primitive form of a human drives the Yekubian to suicide: "On all earth, living creatures rend one another, and feast with unutterable cruelty on their kith and kin" (521). Thus Long ends with Campbell reigning as a Yekubian more "benevolently than any man of earth had ever ruled an empire of men" (521).

Significant critiques from many fans and scholars are that Howard's contribution seems implausible, if not preposterous, given that the physical actions and heroics may not even be possible with the centipede-like form of a Yekubian, coupled with criticism of Long's semi-abandonment of the narrative by seemingly acquiescing to both Howard's and Lovecraft's worldviews. Lovecraft, however, retains the upper hand and his cosmic vision outlasts them both. The thematic conclusion to Lovecraft narratives that endures is the change into a new life form, a metamorphosis of some type ultimately embraced by the protagonist. That is the fate of George Campbell, subverting the narrative intentions of the other contributors. Transformation—transcendence—acceptance.

Works Cited

de Camp, L. Sprague. *Lovecraft: A Biography*. Garden City, NY: Doubleday, 1975.

Joshi, S. T. "Barbarism vs. Civilization: Robert E. Howard and H. P. Lovecraft in Their Correspondence." In *Lovecraft and a World in Transition: Collected Essays on H. P. Lovecraft*. New York: Hippocampus Press, 2014. 73–96.

Lovecraft, H. P. ["Notes to 'The Challenge from Beyond.'"] In *Collected Essays, Volume 5: Philosophy; Autobiography & Miscellany*. Ed. S. T. Joshi. New York: Hippocampus Press, 2006. 257–59.

———. *Selected Letters V*. Ed. August Derleth and James Turner. Sauk City, WI: Arkham House, 1976.

———, and Robert E. Howard. *A Means to Freedom: The Letters of H. P. Lovecraft and Robert E. Howard*. Ed. S. T. Joshi, David E. Schultz, and Rusty Burke. New York: Hippocampus Press, 2009. 2 vols.

——— et al. "The Challenge from Beyond." In Lovecraft's *Collected Fiction: A Variorum Edition, Volume 4: Revisions and Collaborations*. New York: Hippocampus Press, 2017. 503–21.

Finding the Everything in Nothing

Christopher Ropes

SIMON STRANTZAS. *Nothing Is Everything*. Pickering, ON: Undertow Publications, 2018. 274 pp. $17.99 tpb. ISBN: 978-1-988964-03-4.

I have struggled with severe depression all of my life and taken many meds to try to control it. Some of these medications did not do precisely what they were supposed to do. I've had medications cause anxiety attacks, panic attacks, and worsening suicidal thinking. But one of the medications did . . . something else.

Sitting in my room, on my bed and reading a book, I noticed that something felt off somehow. The walls and nightstand and the book in my hands and even my hands themselves seemed to lack solidity or familiarity. It was a little like the old joke about someone stealing everything the comedian owned and replacing it all with exact duplicates. Except, in my case, they'd stolen everything I owned and replaced it with shadowy, insubstantial duplicates. It was a harrowing experience, and this brush with the powers of a psychoactive substance to alter one's entire sense of reality was very similar to my experience reading Simon Strantzas's *Nothing Is Everything*.

The stories in the book, almost without exception, contain a variation on the title somewhere in the text. This device gives a sense of cohesion to the collection. Another tactic Strantzas uses to great effect is his focus on women protagonists. I applaud Strantzas for giving such a powerful voice to women in this collection and with such a degree of success. Only when looking at my notes later did I realize this is what he'd done. It wasn't a belabored point within the book.

The stories themselves are individual gems with mind-bending powers, each one a standout but still contributing to an overall impact that sustained the book throughout. The overall sense of the stories is of reality itself steadily eroding to reveal an inner world of seemingly ordinary women that dove-tails with hidden entities and forces beyond the façade of the mundane. In societies where women's experiences often count for nothing, within these pages that nothingness is absolutely everything.

"In this Twilight," the first tale, takes its title from a Nine Inch Nails song and, if you read the lyrics to the song, you can find echoes of them in the story. Melancholy Harriet is a compelling main character who (perhaps) meets one possible narrator for Trent Reznor's lyrics. A recurring theme in this book causes me to see many connections with Richard Gavin's books. In Gavin's stories there is usually a secret hidden behind the face of the ordinary. The impact in both Gavin's and Strantzas's stories comes from a confrontation with that occulted se-cret. While much of what happens to the main characters could be termed horrific, I feel a better word for the impossible-to-predict endings to be "revelatory." In this book, all the pro-tagonists eventually find a place by the end of their stories where they can say, "Nothing is everything," with a unique inflection, specific to their own humanity and experiences.

"Our Town's Talent" is a beautifully shocking feminist horror masterpiece. It is told in a fashion reminiscent of a Thomas Ligotti story. There is a narrator who clearly is a part of "our town" but is never specifically identified, and who tells the events in an almost dispassionate way. One could argue, in this story as well as most of the others, whether the horror ac-tually involves anything "bad" or if it seems horrific because of the otherworldly, awe-inspiring nature of the events.

"These Last Embers," a lush autumnal tale, takes us into the tragedy of Samantha's family and explores the radical transfor-mations that are sometimes the counterpart to reunion.

"The Flower Unfolds" is where I really became almost overwhelmed by Strantzas's gifts. This story is a look at a beaten-down woman, crushed by society and her corporate environment, until she is escorted by a strange man to her of-fice building's botanical gardens. The writing here almost in-duced a kind of ecstasy in me. Prose, as fragrant as the flowers and as lyrical as their forms, carries along a look at Candice's sexual and emotional liberation from her stultifying work and repressed life.

One of the longest stories in the book, "Ghost Dogs" is a triumphant anchor in the book's center. It elegantly leads you into layer upon layer of mystery about the dystopian world the unnamed narrator inhabits. Is it a terrible future or an alternate present? The loss and sorrow in this story spill out from the pages and lap at the very fingertips of the reader. The narrator is dismantled piece-by-piece until all that remains is her obsessive and explicitly self-destructive need to see the titular ghost dogs. Her need to escape the despair of living in Whitby and her desperation that someone, anyone be different from the people she's known her entire life will resonate deeply with anyone who has ever felt trapped by a location, by their own friends and family, by the entirety of their lives.

"In the Tall Grass" is perhaps not the most Aickmanesque tale here, but it perfectly demonstrates Robert Aickman's idea that a strange story most closely resembles a poem. A truly lyrical exploration of grief and motherhood, this is an odd and impossible to categorize shaft of pain lancing the reader's heart.

I almost see a retelling of the Pandora's Box myth in "The Fifth Stone," except, instead of being a "curiosity killed the cat" moral, it confronts the idea of "Is it even fair to expect someone to hold back the horrors of the world?" The narrator in this story is the character in this book I most identified with, and this is perhaps my personal favorite. Much of my own life, including psychiatric meds and the unfair responsibility of controlling a condition I never asked for, spoke deeply to me.

Another story that felt a good deal like a Thomas Ligotti story to me, with much less cynical despair and a lot more concern for the impact of human relationships, is "The Terrific Mr. Toucan." A married couple go to see a magician and learn that we don't ever know what (or who) we think we know and that true magic is always someone a relationship between ourselves and other beings.

"Alexandra Lost" is another riff on a song, this one I'm much more familiar with than the Nine Inch Nails track we began with. "Alexandra Leaving" is a perfect slice of melancholy from Leonard Cohen, who makes a kind of appearance in the story as Alexandra's partner. Read the lyrics to the song on Google, and it still won't prepare you for what happens when Alexandra leaves "with her lord."

The closing novella, "All Reality Blossoms in Flames," is the ruby-red, diamond-hard, crystalline pure soul of the collection. The main character, Mae, is caught up with some "art terrorists" and comes face-to-face with a completely unexpected insight into the nature of art itself. This story was like my medication experience more than any of the others. For the majority of the tale, I wasn't sure whether weird elements would even appear. I won't spoil any of the surprises along the way, but Mae's joy in the beauty of art, her ponderings about what art means, and her passion for being an artist will speak to any creators of art. But what that voice is saying . . . only Strantzas can tell you that.

Ultimately, the experience of reading *Nothing Is Everything* is the experience of seeing a master live out the Robert Aickman concept I mentioned above. These are works of literary horror or weird fiction that can also be seen as poems, as lyrical examinations of universal human experiences that cause us to see those emotions and sensations from a new vantage point. Revelations pile on revelations, beautiful words paint beautiful pictures of beautiful people undergoing unearthly but still beautiful transformations. *Nothing Is Everything* is an early contender for my favorite horror/weird fiction collection of the year.

Weird Fiction and Decadence

S. T. Joshi

JAMES MACHIN. *Weird Fiction in Britain 1880–1939*. London & New York: Palgrave Macmillan, 2018. ix, 259 pp. $84.99 hc. ISBN: 978-3-319-90526-6.

The title of this book is a bit misleading, for it is neither an historical study of the period in question nor a critical analysis of the major weird writers who were active at this time, but a little bit of both. What Machin, a visiting lecturer at the Royal College of Art, seeks to establish is that weird fiction grew out of (or was at least influenced by) the Decadent movement in England during the 1890s, as well as by a countervailing movement that expanded upon the rugged, "manly" adventure fiction of H. Rider Haggard and other nineteenth-century authors. Weird fiction also straddled the distinction between "high" and "low" literature that was becoming increasingly pronounced (although still somewhat muddled) during this time, as the radical advance of literacy entailed by educational reforms in the later nineteenth century bred a reaction on the part of some highbrow authors who sought to cater only to the refined tastes of a select coterie.

In his somewhat meandering introduction, Machin focuses on both the etymology of the term "weird" (originally a noun—*wyrd*—meaning one's personal destiny or fate) and its increasing use during the mid-nineteenth century. The terms "weird fiction" and "weird tale" emerged at this time, occurring even in titles such as Charlotte Riddell's *Weird Stories* (1882) and J. Sheridan Le Fanu's posthumous *The Watcher and Other Weird Stories* (1894). Elsewhere in his introduction, Machin clarifies the scope of his study. He will, for instance, not cover the Victorian ghost story—a wise decision, I think, since this subgenre has already been widely discussed in previous scholarship and to my mind is not likely to yield fruitful results. Machin also eschews the pure fantasy work of Lord

Dunsany and others, in spite of the fact that Dunsany himself has some slight connection (via the illustrations of S. H. Sime, one of which—for Machen's *House of Souls*—is reproduced here) to the Decadent movement.

In chapter one, "Weird Fin-de-Siècle and After," Machin studies the influence of the *Yellow Book,* published by John Lane, on weird fiction, although strangely he does not provide much analysis of the prototypical fusion of Decadence and the weird at this juncture, Wilde's *The Picture of Dorian Gray* (1890). But Machin keenly observes that the sensational 1895 trial and subsequent imprisonment that destroyed Wilde's reputation and led to his early death did not in fact result in a collapse of the Decadent movement in England. John Lane continued to publish notable works of both Decadent and weird fiction in its Keynotes series (including two books by Arthur Machen), in spite of the hostility to it exhibited by conservative critics. Machin of course resurrects the figure of Max Nordau, whose notorious treatise *Degeneration* (1892) was used as a stick with which to beat any writers or artists who ventured beyond conventional Victorian pieties; but Machin also unearths a lesser-known figure, Harry Quilter, a "belligerent art critic" who not only attacked Arthur Machen's "The Great God Pan" in 1895 but even labelled the seemingly wholesome Sir Arthur Conan Doyle as "morbid, painful, and depressing"!

Machin now turns his attention to three relatively obscure figures—M. P. Shiel, Eric, Count Stenbock, and R. Murray Gilchrist. He recognizes that these authors are obscure and perhaps do not provide much grist for the critic; indeed, his study of Gilchrist (author of the eccentric story collection *The Stone Dragon* [1894]) largely consists of a summary of his reputation. I also feel that Machin could have done much more with Shiel; there is insufficient analysis of Shiel's two great tales, "Vaila" (later rewritten as "The House of Sounds") and "Xélucha," to say nothing of *The Purple Cloud* (1901; revised 1930), perhaps still the greatest "last man on earth" book ever written. A section on "Weird Orientalism" shows how weird writers drew upon the *Arabian Nights,* Beckford's *Vathek,* and other texts to create weird "Arabian Tales." But in the course of this discussion Machin commits the startling gaffe of asserting that Lovecraft's *Necronomicon* was inspired by Robert W. Chambers's *The King in Yellow*—an assertion that was already being ridiculed when Lin Carter made it in *Lovecraft: A Look Behind the Cthulhu Mythos* (1972). It has been known for decades that Lovecraft did not read *The King in Yellow* until 1927, years after he had already cited the *Necronomicon* in "The Hound" (1922) and other tales.

This chapter also focuses on Arthur Machen, who is by no means little known; indeed, Machin chides a number of contemporary commentators for overemphasizing Machen's obscurity—as when Damien G. Walter, as late as 2009, published an article in the London *Guardian* titled "Machen Is the Forgotten Father of Weird Fiction." Machin draws upon the recent publication of *Arthur Machen's 1890s Notebook* (2016) to demonstrate Machen's absorption of Decadent works of this period, including Pierre Louÿs's scandalous novel *Aphrodite* (1896).

But Machin engages in a somewhat tendentious defense of Machen, who has been accused of being a misogynist in the portrayal of Helen Vaughan in "The Great God Pan." I think this is a case of Machin protesting a bit too much. He rightly maintains that Helen's descent into protoplasmic slime at the end of the story is not in itself evidence of misogyny, since Francis Leicester suffers a similar fate in "Novel of the White Powder," with no one accusing Machen of prejudice against men; but, on the other side, the fact that Machen had two apparently happy marriages to women who were hardly models of Victorian passivity and obsequiousness is not particularly compelling evidence that he was *not* a misogynist. Machin pointedly fails to note an earlier passage in "The Great God Pan," where a succession of fops in London commit suicide as a result of encounters with Helen—and the narrative clearly blames her for their dire fates. (It is precisely this aspect of the story that Peter Straub adapted for his novel *Ghost Story* [1979], which is why *that* work is also open to accusations of misogyny.)

Still, the claim that Machen was a misogynist may be somewhat exaggerated; but Machin goes on to criticize several critics (including myself) for maintaining that the story also reveals a "horror of aberrant sex" (my formulation). Machin curiously accuses me of "circular reasoning" because I drew upon Lovecraft's comment—written years after his overly effusive paean to Machen in "Supernatural Horror in Literature"—that Machen was one of those people who "take the artificial and obsolete concept of 'sin' seriously, and find it full of dark allurement." This is quite an astute observation. Lovecraft is emphasizing that the religious orthodoxy that Machen retained for the whole of his life impelled him to lash out at any tendencies that might cause that orthodoxy to crumble. Machin seriously undervalues the role of Machen's religious beliefs in the formation of his fiction. He rightly notes that Machen violently objected to the advance of science—but fails to add that Machen's great fear was that science would introduce an age of widespread secularism that would render his own brand of Anglo-Catholicism obsolete.

In particular, Machin fails to note Machen's highly ambiguous attitude toward paganism—an important component of the Decadent worldview. In a later chapter Machin actually quotes a 1908 article by Machen in which he lambastes his contemporaries for believing that "good pagans could do exactly what they pleased" (i.e., they are not bound by Christian orthodoxy); he lists several examples ("drinking Falernian wine," etc.), the last being "enjoying themselves in other agreeable fashions." This allusion to sexual license is vital, because it is really the basis of the horror in both "The Great God Pan" and also "The White People"—a work that, although it is clearly the pinnacle of Machen's weird writing, Machin incredibly never even mentions. In effect, Machen's loathing of sexual activity outside the bounds of Christian marriage led him to create a body of weird fiction that strove, in effect, to frighten his readers back to orthodoxy. In this way he unwittingly anticipated the Catholic William Peter Blatty, who in *The Exorcist* (1971) and other novels had exactly the same agenda.

The author who receives the greatest attention in this book is John Buchan, who cannot be said to occupy a very significant place in the weird fiction of this period. Machin notes that Buchan—who has frequently been dismissed as merely an adventure writer, and a jingoistic imperialist to boot—is now receiving renewed critical attention; but his analysis seems unfocused and does not justify the space it occupies in the book. Still, Machin provides valuable insights by drawing upon documents from the archives of the publisher John Lane, where the young Buchan served as an evaluator of manuscripts, several of them weird. Buchan reveals both an acuity in his analysis of the works in question and a keen sense of their market potential. But even after Machin's sporadic discussion of Buchan's weird work, I remain unconvinced that he is in any way a significant figure in the field, although Machin has unearthed what may be a forgotten gem, the novel *The Dancing Floor* (1926).

The final chapter in this book focuses on, of all things, the pulp magazine *Weird Tales.* No one needs to be told that this was an American magazine with largely American contributions; and Machin is not at all convincing in asserting that it extended the fusion of Decadence with adventure fiction that he sees in earlier British work. Machin is forced to study the classic reprints in the magazine (which, very sporadically, did include works such as Gautier's "Clarimonde" and Robert W. Chambers's "The Demoiselle d'Ys"), but he will need a lot more than this to prove his case. Still, he has done interesting work in dredging up comments by readers suggesting that they recognized at least some of the original works appearing in the magazine (especially by Lovecraft, Clark Ashton Smith, and other notables) were genuine contributions to literature and not just pulp rubbish (as, frankly, most of the contents of the magazine were). But I for one would have preferred a critic of Machin's perspicacity to focus on actual (and meritorious) British writing of the early decades of the twentieth century, ranging from Robert Hichens to Oliver Onions to Walter de la Mare to L. P. Hartley, and especially to Algernon Blackwood, a titan if ever there was one. Works by a few of these authors are discussed briefly; others are not mentioned at all.

There are other small blemishes in Machin's book. He seems to have a bit of a problem with names. We find Laird "Baron" (for Barron), Edith "Birkenhead" (for Birkhead, the pioneering author of *The Tale of Terror,* 1921), and, most inexcusably, Friedrich "Nietzche" (for Nietzsche). We read that Lord Dunsany was the "18th Baron *of* Dunsany" (the "of" is erroneous and supernumerary). Machin misspells the title of Buchan's "The Green Wildebeest" as ". . . Wildebeeste"—then implicitly criticizes Lovecraft for spelling the title correctly! And Machin takes an almost perverse delight in writing "who" when "whom" is grammatically required, and also writes "neither . . . or" for "neither . . . nor." When such a prodigiously learned Englishman is so slovenly with the English language, what hope is there? (More to the point: where were the publisher's copy editors and fact checkers?) Moreover, Machin is always on the verge of lapsing into obfuscatory lit crit jargon; he has a peculiar fondness for the verb "imbricate" (which, I find, means "to arrange (sc. scales) so that they overlap like roof tiles") and its cognates. He regularly uses the term "anthology" (a volume of stories by many different writers) when he means "collection" (a volume of stories by a single writer).

I do not wish to create a false impression of this book. It is an occupational hazard of book reviewers to nitpick, and I have probably done more of it than I should have. Let me therefore declare that this book is unquestionably a significant contribution to the study of weird fiction, and even those well-versed in the literature of the period would benefit from reading it. There is some illuminating nugget—whether it be a contemporary review, a little-known comment by an author on his or her work, or a penetrating assessment by Machin himself—on nearly every page, and throughout we can easily detect Machin's enthusiasm for his subject, and his determination to establish weird fiction in general, as well as certain authors in particular, firmly within the canon of English literature. Discursive as his analysis at times is, it is safe to say that he has succeeded in this task.

That Is Not How the Story Goes

Bev Vincent

THEODORA GOSS. *Snow White Learns Witchcraft: Stories and Poems.* n.p.: Mythic Delirium Books, 2019. 224 pp. $15.95 tpb. ISBN: 978-1-7326440-0-7.

Anyone who has read the original Grimm's *Fairy Tales* knows that things don't play out the way they do in the Disney versions. Fairy tales are, indeed, grim, and characters do not always come to happy endings. Disney, for example, doesn't show the evil queen being forced to dance to her death in hot iron shoes.

Theodora Goss read Hungarian legends as a girl and now teaches fairy tales to students at Boston University. In this collection, she re-imagines familiar stories and creates new ones, sometimes laying bare the truth of the classic tales, occasionally imbuing them with a feminist perspective. Even as the subjects of tales, women were often regarded as trophies for princes in the old legends. Goss demonstrates that things that seem magical in a fairy tale might not be so attractive in the cold light of reality.

These are stories and poems of love, greed, jealousy, and revenge. Are there monsters? Certainly: trolls (not all of them evil), dragons, witches, wolves, and other creatures of the night. There are also talking cats, bears, and wolves. There's even a dash of cannibalism in the poem about "The Ogress Queen," who salivates as she speculates about what her husband's illegitimate children might taste like with a glass of Riesling.

The title poem, which opens the collection, sets the tone. Snow White, now older and a mother, has avoided asking the famous question of the all-knowing mirror she inherited—a question that, when asked by an evil witch (her mother) many years earlier, unleashed a series of events that shaped the course of her life. Living with seven dwarves is not as romantic as it sounds, and her prince of a husband turned out to be worse than useless. Snow White never forgave him for how he punished the witch. It is a poem about empowerment: she shuns the jealousy that destroyed her mother, and now that her husband is dead she plans to become a witch, "the only role [old women] get to write yourself."

The tales are set in places from the classic "land far away" to fictional Eastern European kingdoms to Boston, and in times ranging from "once upon a time" to the twentieth century to the Facebook era. Often the works in this collection break the fourth wall: several characters are aware that they are living in a fairy tale. In "Red as Blood and White as Bone," a girl who was once part of a fairy tale grows up wanting to preserve them.

There are recurring elements, often in stories and poems that are grouped together. There is a "rose" cycle, stories about witches and wolves, two different views of Rumpelstiltskin and three of Little Red Riding Hood (the woodsman is a kind of wolf, and maybe she is, too), as well as several poems about women who marry bears. There are toads in need of kissing and witches disguised as seemingly innocuous old women.

In several works, Goss extrapolates the lives of familiar characters. What was the rest of her life like for the little mermaid who gave up her voice for legs to dwell with mankind on dry land ("Conversations with the Sea Witch")? How did Goldilocks turn out after her encounter with the three bears ("Goldilocks and the Bear")?

The standout story in the collection, "Blanchefleur," loosely inspired by the classic "The White Cat," is about Ivan, the son of a mortal and a fairy who is treated like the village idiot after his mother dies and his devastated father ignores his upbringing. Ivan's maternal aunt volunteers to apprentice him for three years; in fact, she lends him to three different individuals for one-year periods of servitude: an owl who helps compile an encyclopedia, a lizard who is a travel writer, and a pack of wolves who defend against marauding trolls. From each of these experiences he gains valuable wisdom and, more importantly, talismans that will serve him during his adult years as his destiny is fulfilled.

Another noteworthy piece is "The Other Thea," in which a young woman discovers that she needs to retrieve her shadow, which her grandmother stole from her years earlier, or else she will fade away. To do so, she must travel to the Other Country and put into practice many of the things she learned at the School of Witchcraft. In "A Country Called Winter," the protagonist, who emigrated from a mystical (and mythical) European country when she was young, embraces her status as an American citizen before learning that the past is not yet finished with her.

The stories do not all have resolutions. "The Rose in Twelve Petals" retells "Sleeping Beauty," even bringing in the perspectives of the fateful spinning wheel and the castle tower where everyone slept for a hundred years. What happened when they awakened? After revealing her preferred outcome, the narrator admits that she is still waiting to find out what will really transpire.

Purists might insist, as a voice does within this collection, "That is not how the story goes," to which the narrator responds, "But that is how I prefer to tell it." In these stories and poems, Goss demonstrates the power in telling one's own story rather than having it told by someone else.

Sesqua Valley's Weirdest Inhabitant, Wilum Pugmire

David Barker

On 26 March 2019, my dear friend and collaborator, renowned author of Lovecraftian fiction, W. H. Pugmire, passed away. Weird fiction has lost a master craftsman, and a truly good person. Lovecraft scholar S. T. Joshi said that Wilum was "the prose-poet of the horror/fantasy field; he may be the best prose-poet we have." I will miss Wilum terribly, as will his many fans. We won't see another writer that is his equal. His prose is exotic, evocative, sensual, and emotional. Many of his pieces are set in his invented realm of Sesqua Valley, where most of the inhabitants are supernatural creatures who are only partly human. The storyline is often vague or even cryptic. Mood matters more than plot. And the Mythos monster is the hero of the tale.

I became friends with Wilum Pugmire around 1988. In those pre-Internet days, horror writers relied on *Scavenger's Newsletter,* Janet Fox's monthly listing of literary markets. That's where I got my start as a horror author. In 1988, I began my own Lovecraftian horror zine, *Midnight Shambler,* and asked for submissions in *Scavenger's.* I received lush, exquisitely crafted prose pieces from a fellow in Seattle named Wilum Hopfrog Pugmire, Esq. His unusual stories were richly atmospheric and beautifully written; I was an instant fan. This was before email, and authors submitted their work by mail with a cover letter. Wilum's letters were delightful. Handwritten on the backs of unused pages from his music zine *Punk Lust,* his penmanship resembled eighteenth-century script, and he dated them back two centuries, as did his hero, H. P. Lovecraft, so that "1988" became "1788."

I published a couple of his stories plus a review that he wrote in the first two issues of *Shambler,* and was planning a special All-Pugmire issue when I abruptly decided to shut down my zine. Thus, the Wilum special issue was cancelled, something I still regret. In 1990 I edited a one-off zine on the centennial of HPL's birth called *The Lovecrafter—100th Anniversary Edition,* and Wilum had a piece in that. He published one of my stories in his zine, *Tales of Lovecraftian Horror.* Although I never met him in person back then, I considered Wilum a friend. In the late 1990s, I drifted away from the horror scene and lost touch with Wilum, although I continued to write weird stories that I made no attempt to publish.

In early 2012 I decided to return to horror, and was surprised to see that many of the authors I had known in the small press scene had gone on to establish reputations in the now burgeoning field of professionally published Cthulhu Mythos fiction; Wilum was an important figure among them. His video blogs on YouTube revealed that despite his new celebrity as a leading Lovecraftian author, he had sacrificed none of his originality. He still presented himself as the self-proclaimed "Queen of Eldritch Horror" and obsessed Lovecraft fanboy, dressed in drag with his face painted green or red or yellow, with sigils on his face, wearing a Pope hat featuring a photo of Barbara Streisand, or Boy George, or Poe. Who he was hadn't changed; he had simply become legendary.

Then a friend, Obadiah Baird (editor of *The Audient Void*), bought me a ticket to the 2012 H. P. Lovecraft Film Festival in Portland, Oregon. Wilum gave a reading the day we attended, and I made a point of being there. It was incredible. He read several short pieces, most or all prose poems. After the first one, I whispered to Obadiah, "You can see why I published him—he's great!" The piece that had the strongest impact on me was a melancholy prose poem called "Letters from an Old Gent," in which he imagines Lovecraft visiting his father's grave. He followed that with very poignant comments about what Lovecraft meant to him personally as a writer and said that, due to his poor health, this might be the last year he would attend the Festival.

Afterwards, as he was leaving the auditorium, I timidly approached him and introduced myself, saying, "I don't know if you remember me, but I think I published you many years ago." He did remember me, and gave me a very warm welcome, hugging me. He seemed genuinely moved to meet me, and it was mutual. I introduced Obadiah, and then, not wanting to tire him or take up too much of his time, we left him alone. Ultimately, Wilum and I hung out together at six different cons, all of which were wonderful experiences for me.

Shortly after the 2012 HPLFF, Wilum and I became Facebook friends, and one day he asked me if I had enough Lovecraftian stories to make up a book. I said I did, and he offered to help me find a publisher for that book. I was stunned by his generosity and mailed him manuscripts of ten of my best Lovecraftian tales. Eventually he did interest a publisher in a book that would be half his stories and half mine. Then he suggested we collaborate on a story to spice up the collection. I felt extremely honored that he thought me up to the task. I took this challenge very seriously and gave it my all. In total, we collaborated on five works: the novella *The Revenant of Rebecca Pascal,* the stories "In the Gulfs of Dream" and "The Stairway in the Crypt" from *In the Gulfs of Dream and Other Lovecraftian Tales,* the novel *Witches in Dreamland,* and the poem "Audience at Sunset." Working with an artist of his skill and imagination was a life-changing experience, for which I am deeply grateful.

But Wilum Pugmire was far more than a superb literary artist. He was the sweetest, kindest, most giving person I have ever known. May his memory as a great human being endure forever, and may his stories be cherished by future generations of weird fiction fans.

Ramsey's Rant: Horror versus Horror

Ramsey Campbell

Ever since horror became a defined genre, we've seen struggles between representatives of its extremes. My theory (for which I have no definite evidence) is that Dorothy L. Sayers put together *Great Tales of Detection, Mystery and Horror* (1928 et seq.) as a riposte to the *Not at Night* series. Christine Campbell Thomson declared that in editing *Not at Night* (1925) and its successors, she set her face against literature, and the Sayers volumes look to me like bids to reclaim the field for it. Whereas the Thomson books don't refer to horror as a marketable element until several volumes into the series— and then only in excerpts from reviews—Sayers puts it in her title, where it may be read as a pointed declaration. Her substantial introduction, a history of the detective tale, grows much terser when it comes to horror, but her observation that "each day the public demands a greater subtlety of theme and treatment" may summarise her editorial principles. Oddly, she refers (presumably approvingly) to the "delicious nausea" that the wooing of Professor Guildea may provoke.

1931 saw Montague Summers's *Supernatural Omnibus,* which makes clear that he's countering Thomson. In his fine introduction he convicts her anthologies for a lack of the spiritual and for being nauseating—exactly M. R. James's objection to them. In 1933 Marjorie Bowen gave us *Great Tales of Horror,* placing Pushkin and Gogol alongside Blackwood and Machen. 1934 brought us John Gawsworth's anthology *New Tales of Horror by Eminent Authors,* so strange a book that I'll return to it at length. 1944 was the year of *Great Tales of Terror and the Supernatural,* in which the selection by Phyllis Fraser and Herbert A. Wise succeeds both as literature and horror, earning praise from Edmund Wilson, not least for reviving the public taste for the genre.

I've no basis for claiming that it was designed to demonstrate its literary credentials as well, but I believe John Kier

Cross's *Best Horror Stories* might well have been. This appeared in 1957, not long after horror had attracted such public opprobrium (inflamed by the media) that horror comics were deplored in Parliament, which banned their sale or publication with the 1955 Children and Young Persons (Harmful Publications) Act. In the year the Cross anthology appeared, Hammer Films and their competitors became the next focus for disapproval—indeed, loathing in some quarters—but *Best Horror Stories* appears to have made its case for literature. Besides specialists such as Poe and M. R. James it featured the likes of Graham Greene and Angus Wilson, and was dominated by Herman Melville's "Bartleby." The book, and that inclusion in particular, shaped my view of the field as a writer.

When I came to edit horror anthologies I'm sure the Cross loomed at the back of my mind. In all of them I've tried to demonstrate the scope of the field. To be fair, Herbert van Thal brought some range to the earlier Pan Books of Horror, but by the time I put *Superhorror* together many of his selections were coarsely sadistic, and my book was meant as a response. It didn't succeed with everyone: Richard Geis condemned Brian Lumley's tale for gruesomeness, a comment Robert Aickman found unreasonable. Originally conceived as a *Dangerous Visions* of horror, *New Terrors* let me range wider still in my inclusions, and I stand by every one of them. While some are as quiet as a whisper, they convey insidious disquiet to me.

This brings me back to the curious case of Gawsworth's *New Tales of Horror*. The previous year Marjorie Bowen used Algernon Blackwood's "The Woman's Ghost Story," a gently redemptive tale whose core of terror perhaps justifies its presence in a horror book, but I find it hard if not impossible to understand some of Gawsworth's inclusions. Could they have been written for a different project? I admit this has happened to me. "Another World" was conceived for an anthology of tales about a forbidden planet, not simply stories by some of us who'd signed books at the shop, but Brian Aldiss and I produced our contributions before the concept changed. "Going Under" was intended for an anthology about obsessions rather than dark love, and I recently wrote a tale for a book called *Horrors and Other Peculiarities* with an eye to the latter quality, only for the anthology to be renamed for horror alone. Perhaps Gawsworth pulled his original proposal out from under some of the contributors—I can only wonder. He would subsequently edit three anthologies that announced they offered thrills, but even that term is too strong for some of the *New Tales of Horror*. While the jacket flap promises "many brilliant gems of Horror" and "the greater range of terror's facets," it ends by invoking Edgar Wallace, by whose work it was "impossible not to be thrilled." Such is not the case with too many stories here.

Arthur Machen lends his name but no sense of dread, even though he is represented twice. He contributes a faintly risqué anecdote in which a man's double passes overnight for him, and a trivial tale of a disappearance, where a hint of fear goes undeveloped. Hugh MacDiarmid appears to be a poet turned to prose, which leads in "The Dead Harlot" (a morbid meditation on mortality) to a highly decorated style at the expense of narrative. His tale "A'Body's Lassie" is a folktale of a sprite, told in synthetic dialect that sometimes borders on impenetrability but never yields unease, while "Wound-Pie" applies the same style to a sketchy account of desperate measures rendered comprehensible (and mildly horrific) by the punch line. "The Stranger" resorts to plain prose but takes four pages to confirm what the opening line suggests, without growing any stranger than its title. I gather that MacDiarmid owes his reputation to more substantial work. Too many tales in the book suffer not just from excessive brevity but from disproportion—for instance, Sir Ronald Ross hardly has time to sketch his protagonist before the chap turns homicidal, but with none of the intensity that conciseness afforded to Poe. By contrast, "The House of Dust"—a tale of a familiar sort of ghostly encounter, conventionally developed—takes fifteen pages to demonstrate why Herbert de Hamel is pretty thoroughly forgotten, though Peter Haining reprinted the tale.

Stephen Graham provides an anti-war vignette, or more precisely an anti-German piece, warning of racial supremacism—timely enough at the time, but hardly horror. E. H. W. Meyerstein delivers a lengthily oblique study of a sociopath, faintly hinting at an occult undercurrent, and does produce a chill. By contrast, his confrontation between a parson and a prison warder may make a point but falls short of at least the present commentator. Charles Duff's two contributions are sadly worthy of his surname: his gang of spectral murderers bring too many clichés with them to benefit from a solitary grotesque inspiration (a dance of the hanged), while his tale of a fatal delirium never achieves the conviction it strains for. Herbert Palmer provides a perfunctory prophetic dream that fails to put on flesh. The book ends with Marcus Magill's violent tale of a perfect murder gone wrong—suspenseful but a little short of horror.

Let me not imply that the book is entirely unrewarding or unworthy of its title. Richard Middleton contributes two uncommonly unsparing accounts of murder bordering on if not entering the psychopathic, and a tale of a ghastly seduction, as well as a terse bleak glimpse of an afterlife, all of which make up for his longest tale here, little more than a practical joke. E. H. Visiak seems to refer to his remarkable novel *Medusa* in "Medusan Madness," which offers a vision of perhaps related strangeness. Gawsworth himself provides a distillation of sylvan fear reminiscent of Blackwood. Frederick Carter offers two versions of a grisly situation, along with a tale of a jape that drives its victim to violence and a nightmarish encounter with masks. R. L. Mégroz has a striking idea, perhaps even original at the time—a stray broadcast that comes from the future—and evokes a frisson of dread. Nugent Barker very gradually reveals the horrid secret of his tale. He is one of the few actual masters of horror among the contributors, and certainly delivers more of it than Machen does here.

I've left one name until last, although he doesn't occupy that position. M. P. Shiel was celebrated by Lovecraft for his finest work. "The Globe of Gold-fish" is a minor tale of murder, but "How Life Climbs" is something else. I can't call it science fiction—even science fantasy stretches the first word close to snapping—but its account of an encounter with an alien spacecraft and its occupants is remarkable nonetheless, not to say stylistically efflorescent. Most of twenty years later Philip José Farmer would be hailed for tackling the theme of alien sex, but Shiel does that here, involving multiple participants (and splendidly describing sperm as a "dashing gang of gallants"). Would it have been read as horror when it was published? It is certainly ahead of its time, and is among the reasons why the anthology is worth tracking down for the best of its unreprinted contents. Despite its proportion of failures, I celebrate its ambition and scope.

Marvelous Milicent: The Rise and Removal of a Monster-Artist Maven

Danel Olson

MALLORY O'MEARA. *The Lady from the Black Lagoon: Hollywood Monsters and the Lost Legacy of Milicent Patrick*. Toronto: Hanover Square Press, 2019. 366 pp. $26.99 hc. ISBN: 978-1-335-93780-3.

For those who appreciate distance between biographers and their subjects, *The Lady from the Black Lagoon: Hollywood Monsters and the Lost Legacy of Milicent Patrick* will appall. For others who want to learn the furtive life of the subject and feel the biographer's admiration as she follows her muse's trail, learning how sexism and harassment have inescapably impacted both, Malloy O'Meara's first published book will impress. The book O'Meara gives us is an entertaining hybrid: a biography of Milicent Patrick along with O'Meara's personal story and her general look at the difficulties women face in Hollywood. O'Meara has a self-declared "nerd" fascination with monsters and *fantastika,* evidenced by her associate production for the fantasy/horror comedy *Kids vs. Monsters* (2015) from director Sultan Saeed Al Darmakisulta (who created the film consortium Dark Dunes Productions) and acting as one of the seven producers for another Dark Dunes project, the animated adventure fantasy *Yamasong: March of the Hollows* (2017, directed by Sam Koji Hale). Those two experiences shepherding movies help give O'Meara special insight into where a movie goes all right or all wrong. She loves her things freakish and has an attuned sense for the parts that thousands of crew members each play in a creature feature.

This knowledge helps her assuredly sort through the contributions and rivalries on the set for *The Creature from the Black Lagoon* (1954), which O'Meara first viewed (in absolute awe) at the age of seventeen. The central conflict of the biography surrounds the reported jealousy at Universal Studios (which gave us the Wolfman, Dracula, Frankenstein's creature, King Kong, the Mummy, and more) manifesting from the admittedly talented head of the makeup shop, Bud Westmore, directed toward Milicent Patrick, who sketched the sublime designs for the Creature. Eaten by envy, Westmore would ultimately blackball Milicent for daring to let her imagination bloom. Universal knew it and did nothing to shield her or discipline Westmore.

Westmore himself was part of four fascinating and hyper-competitive generations of makeup and wig designers who served Hollywood brilliantly since 1917, led by their English-immigrant patriarch, George Westmore. The father rose to prominent recognition in the movies (even fashioning Mary Pickford's fattish curls), only to die as a suicide at fifty-two from mercury poisoning. The endless striving among the surviving sons conditioned Bud Westmore, the book alleges, to bleed anyone who might cut into his reputation. O'Meara contends that "during the months [Milicient] was away [on a publicity tour for *Creature*], a storm of resentment and jealousy raged back at the studio . . . By the time she returned to Hollywood, . . . [Westmore] pulled her from the film projects she had already started working on and refused to hire her for future work." In the end, as O'Meara reminds us, Bud Westmore got sole on-screen credit for the iconic amphibian man.

This is the bad blood at the heart of this book: how Milicent as an animator and creature-designer beginning to capture the world's imagination is cut from the vine early by spiteful and intimidated men. O'Meara concentrates on this episode to profile personal cases of how this unfairness goes on against female artists and actors today, establishing the book's #MeToo consciousness. The question, of course (and one that readers might like to have heard more about), is how to fight back most effectively at that kind of disabling sexism that dooms careers, causes PTSD, and diminishes film for us all, makers and viewers.

The rest of the narrative is largely a search for what happened to Milicent after her exile from Universal's drawing department. In this regard, the narrative focuses more on O'Meara and her own journey, and the reader is treated to

O'Meara's meetings with random strangers in stranger places, pressing ever closer to the mysteries of Milicent. But it is a meeting with Milicent's niece Gwen that creates the most emotion. O'Meara learns that Milicent's family thought her a Hollywood whore and largely dismissed her. The artist's last words, according to Gwen, were "God doesn't love me."

Much is to be savored in the odyssey searching for the lost "Millie," the artist-actress who "looked like a goth Jessica Rabbit." I understand that some readers might be put off by the lack of photographs from the journey, the chattiness of the trips, and by how much of the book becomes about O'Meara herself: tattoos she has, including one of Milicent on her arm, the boredom of working from home, the search and desire to acquire a new persona, how pretty Milicent was and what sexy clothes she wore, and righteous anger: "It took me a long time to forgive Milicent. I wanted her to demand Bud Westmore's head on a pike. . . . She should have fought back, she should have, she should have, she should have." Moreover, the book suffers from no index, no maps or illustrations, and almost no parenthetical documentation internally or in the footnotes showing where evidence comes to support O'Meara's history and claims.

On the other hand, there are towering works of the latter kind that do have plentiful personal asides by the biographer and sometimes a conversational tone and a journey to boot. *The Immortal Life of Henrietta Lacks* (2010), which I teach to college students, is certainly one of those first-book biographies where the author winds her personal story, educational experiences, travels, and family meetings with profiteer science and the subject's sad tale. Biographer Rebecca Skloot first hears in a community college biology class of the remarkably reproductive HeLa cells from the cancer victim Ms. Lacks—cells that quietly made billions of dollars for Johns Hopkins University, which grew "fifty million metric tons" of the cells and sold them to universities and drug companies for experimentation without giving her family recompense. This starts her crafting a searching biography that, like O'Meara's, ultimately muses on the exploitation of a woman. *The Immortal Life of Henrietta Lacks* would spend seventy-five weeks on the *New York Times* bestseller list, be taught at over 125 universities, and inspire a movie.

Much of O'Meara's biography is about people's physical appearance, and the effect that striking looks have upon us. But I am mistaken if I argue that O'Meara identifies only with Milicent and is spellbound by her visage only. Perhaps the more moving identification she has is for the man-fish's look of love:

> The Creature watches Kay [actress Julie Adams] from the watery depths, looking up at her with such longing and sadness that it's hard to remember that it's just a rubber mask and not a fully articulated facial makeup. Instead of feeling like a frightened victim [of the lagoon,] . . . you start to remember moments in your life when you were in the role of the Creature. . . . Covered in acne, awkward, feeling fat and ugly, I [in teenage years] didn't know how to approach people I found attractive. I looked at them in my high school hallways the same way that the Creature looked at Kay. Thanks to my generalized anxiety disorder, my palms were also of the same level of clamminess [as the creature's webbed claws].

In this moment of instant empathy and understanding during her first viewing of the Creature, O'Meara bares her emotional depths and remembered shame, unlocking why some horror and fantasy films (e.g., James Whale's *Frankenstein* [1931]) have such potent, unconscious, continued resonance: we are the monster.

For some literary adaptors of creatures, such as Bram Stoker, there are new biographies every year, often incisive and elegantly written by the loveliest minds (cf. David J. Skal, Elizabeth Miller, Dacre Stoker, Catherine Wynne, Lisa Hopkins, Andrew Maunder, et al.). For artists of film monsters like Milicent Patrick (who also drew the famed Xenomorph for 1953's *It Came from Outer Space*), there seem to be so few. *The Lady from the Black Lagoon* is not without its drowning moments: in content, sometimes O'Meara confesses she may overshare, "shooting her Feminist Laser Beams too much"; in tone, sometimes she drops from an elevated film-academic's height to her alter ego's "badass" grunty crassness: "Holy shit.

Telling Milicent's story required a lot of help." Her volume is still appreciated, though, partly because of the paucity of sources on the subject. O'Meara, fiercely attached to Milicent as a creative force and as a symbol of women everywhere sabotaged at their workplace who had such rare gifts to offer us, should be commended for its story. I hope her book—as well as memorable earlier pieces by others like Vincent Di Fate's long illustrated feature "The Fantastic Mystery of Milicent Patrick" for Tor.com (2011)—will inspire more meditation into the life and art of the woman who created an icon and a dream in the water (and why such creators do not get more credit). Guillermo del Toro's amphibian man is analyzed in my own book (a strangely lonely and erotic being conjured by Oscar-worthy Mike Hill, magically acted by Oscar-worthy Doug Jones, and inspired by Milicent Patrick's own genius hand). Del Toro tweeted the last, best word on her the same year his *The Shape of Water* premiered: "A moment of gratitude towards Millicent Patrick—creator extraordinaire."

Maybe Johnny is an Old One?: *The Room* as Lovecraftian Pastiche

Edward Guimont

In 2003, an independent movie named *The Room* debuted in a single theater in Los Angeles, generating $1,800 in ticket sales in two weeks before it was pulled from screening. It was memorably reviewed as "the *Citizen Kane* of bad movies" and its director, writer, producer, and star—a long-haired man with a lazy eye and inscrutable accent named Tommy Wiseau, universally referred to simply as "Tommy"—was hailed as "the Orson Welles of crap." Fast-forward to 2018, and *The Room* routinely plays to sold-out midnight screenings worldwide and has more than recouped its $6,000,000 production budget. Tommy, now something of a celebrity, has appeared on-stage at the Golden Globes and Independent Spirit Awards.

The enduring popularity of *The Room* comes partly from its promotion by celebrities, and partly from how earnestly Tommy made his exceedingly melodramatic film—and how unsuccessfully he was able to convey his intended emotions. The central plot of *The Room* is simple enough. It is the story of Johnny (Tommy), a San Francisco banker engaged to Lisa (Juliette Danielle). Lisa decides to have an affair with Johnny's best friend, Mark, played by Tommy's real-life best (and perhaps only) friend, Greg Sestero. This betrayal ultimately leads Johnny to commit suicide, but not before a tangled series of unrelated events, including Johnny and Mark capturing a drug dealer targeting Johnny's college-aged ward; Lisa's friends repeatedly breaking into Johnny's apartment to have sex on his couch; and Lisa's mother being diagnosed with breast cancer. Johnny ends a business talk with an abrupt change of topic: "Anyway, how is your sex life?" Mark goes from trying to throw his friend Peter (Kyle Vogt) off a rooftop to confiding his secrets to him several seconds later. In one of the most (in)famous scenes, Johnny screams out, "You are tearing me apart, Lisa!" after his "future wife" accuses him of hitting her, but before offering her the reassuring, "Don't worry about it."

While the main inspirations for *The Room* were *The Talented Mr. Ripley, A Streetcar Named Desire,* and *Rebel without a Cause,* it has more often been compared to the films featured on *Mystery Science Theater 3000*—whose cast released their own RiffTrax roast of *The Room* in 2009, as one of several events that year which helped launch *The Room* to its stratospheric heights of popularity. In 2013, Sestero published *The Disaster Artist* [*TDA*], a tell-all book about both the production of *The Room* and his friendship with Tommy; it was in turn made into a 2017 film of the same name, starring James and Dave Franco as Tommy and Sestero. *TDA* remains one of the most in-depth sources on the actual character and history of Tommy, especially before *The Room's* 2009 breakout as a pop-culture phenomenon.

On the surface level, there would not seem to be many connections between Tommy Wiseau, *The Room,* and the works of H. P. Lovecraft. Indeed, a cursory Google search indicates only two direct links. One is a 2009 review of Lovecraft's story "The Other Gods," where the story was considered to be only forgettable in its averageness, as opposed to either good or the "so bad it's good" level of *The Room* (Fifer and Lackey). The second is a 2012 episode of *The Dead Authors Podcast,* where Lovecraft was played by comedian Paul Scheer (Adomian, Scheer, and Tompkins). Scheer subsequently appeared in several movies and podcasts with Tommy. Scheer also co-wrote the 2016 comic *Spider-Man/Deadpool Vol 1. #12,* which briefly established that both Tommy and *The Room* exist within the continuity of Marvel Comics. Direct connections exist, therefore—but are scarce.

It might also be argued that attempting to identify a connection between *The Room* and Lovecraft is frivolous—at best, a joke. Yet would not even this approach be in the spirit of Lovecraft? Stephen Walker has argued that while Lovecraft's greatest contribution was to the horror genre, his "second greatest influence has been on humor. His fiction has created a boutique humor industry (Christmas carols, Cthulhu toys, political slogans, etc.), which subverts horror—itself a subversion—through incongruity" (162). As Arthur C. Clarke himself said of his own 1940 story "At the Mountains of Murki-ness," one of the first works the SF giant ever wrote, "parody is, of course, often the sincerest form of homage" (129).

It is in that spirit of humor—in the shadow of Lovecraft's smile, to paraphrase Walker (151)—that I approach this analysis. Yet despite starting the project with a smile, I believe that not only is there an argument to be made that *The Room* can be seen through a Lovecraftian lens—or, perhaps, shown through a Lovecraftian film projector—but parallels can be drawn between the lives of Lovecraft and Tommy, despite their very different circumstances. It is with the latter connection that I begin.

Author and Auteur: Two Lives in Comparison

For many years, Tommy Wiseau's pre-2003 life was almost impossible to learn about. *The Disaster Artist* reveals some background gleaned by Sestero over the years. The fan documentary *Room Full of Spoons* garnered more, and as a result has been tied up in legal disputes for years with Tommy, who has carefully protected his past and cultivated an air of mystique—much like Wizard Whateley preserving his own family ancestry's secrets in "The Dunwich Horror" (*CF* 2.423). Tommy has always claimed to be from New Orleans; Lovecraft visited the city in 1932, extolling his enjoyment of it in letters to August Derleth and Robert E. Howard (*SL* 4.42–46).

As revealed by Sestero, Tommy did indeed live in New Orleans for a time and enjoyed it as Lovecraft did—but Tommy was actually born in Poznań, Poland, in 1955. As with Lovecraft, Tommy's father died early in his life; unlike Lovecraft, although closer to Derleth, Tommy was a practicing Catholic. Like Lovecraft, Tommy was stridently anti-communist and enchanted with an idealized past version of America—even if for Wiseau the ideal was an Americana 1950s, and for Lovecraft it was the colonial era (*TDA* 192–93). In the early 1970s, Tommy left communist Poland for Strasbourg, France, working in harsh conditions before continuing to Louisiana. It is unlikely that Tommy would have encountered any Lovecraft in communist Poland, as the author was apparently not translated unto Polish until 2007 (Borowska 70). However, in the mid-twentieth century, Polish artist Zdzisław Beksiński created Lovecraft-inspired pieces, some of which were later used as cover art for Lovecraft books. It is also unlikely, but not impossible, that Tommy encountered Lovecraft in Strasbourg, as his translated works were available in France from the end of World War II, and Lovecraftian scholarship was widespread there from 1953 onwards (Spaulding 35–40).

As with Lovecraft, Tommy is a teetotaler (*TDA* 206; *SL* 4.50–51) with strange dietary habits, but a lover of food and eating (*TDA* 48; *SL* 4.102–4). Tommy often feels alienated from society, dislocated, and, at least before his fame hit, was riddled with a lack of belief in himself (*TDA* 187)—again, personality aspects that match Lovecraft (*SL* 4.10–11). As part of his difficult attempts to make friends, Tommy idealizes youth and goes to great lengths to preserve (at least the appearance of) his own, in the hope that he will live for at least two hundred years (*TDA* 79, 121), thus placing him in the company of such Lovecraftian characters as Dr. Muñoz (*CF* 2.15), Herbert West (*CF* 1.319), Ephraim Waite (*CF* 3.347), Joseph Curwen (*CF* 2.351), and even the Cthulhu cult with its belief that "even death may die" (*CF* 2.40).

Nor is his interest in secrecy and youthfulness the only Lovecraftian traits of Tommy's personality. Just as Lovecraft had a childhood interest in the *Arabian Nights* (*SL* 4.8), Tommy is a great fan of the 1992 Disney film *Aladdin* based on the fables (*TDA* 52, 89). Tommy has a habit of drawing the Zodiac Killer's symbol, but claims not to know what it means—in any case, an interest in unknown occult symbols with grisly history is certainly befitting of a Lovecraft character (*TDA* 53)—and the Zodiac itself is evocative of the Lovecraftian waiting for a time when "the stars are right." Tommy's San Francisco apartment is filled with pieces of Aztec art and a bust of Julius Caesar; this is certainly apt not only for Lovecraft's Roman obsession, but his friend R. H. Barlow's later academic career in Aztec studies (*TDA* 54; *SL* 4.332–36). Tommy also has an interest in an imaginary world called Tommy's Planet, which he seems to identify both as an idealized harmonious state for Earth to achieve one day, but also an actual planet in space (*TDA* 59–60). This seems an apt comparison to Yuggoth and its status as both physical planet and (literally) otherworldly realm (*CF* 2.518).

In terms of Tommy's filmmaking, despite the earlier (negative) comparison of him to Orson Welles, he was much more inspired by Alfred Hitchcock (*TDA* 79, 96), the horror director whose arguably greatest film was an adaptation of *Psycho,* written by Lovecraft's friend Robert Bloch. Both Tommy and Sestero have also dabbled in horror films. Sestero appeared in the 1999 *Retro Puppet Master*—a film whose plot included a millennia-old Egyptian sorcerer, shades of Nyarlathotep (*CF* 1.203). Tommy, for his part, appeared in the 2010 short-film horror spoof *The House That Drips Blood on Alex.*

Nor was that short film Tommy's only hope for the horror genre. During the production of *The Room,* Tommy planned on his next film being something called *The Vampire from Alcatraz: King of Vampires.* This interest stemmed not only from the fact that Tommy was sometimes identified as having a certain resemblance to Dracula, but also from his actually believing himself to be a vampire (*TDA* xiii, 50, 84, 139). While vampires were not Lovecraft's usual stock, he did own *Dracula* (Joshi, *Library* 132), discussed vampiric tales in his "Supernatural Horror in Literature" essay (*CE* 2.95–96, 109, 112–13), and drew from the New England vampire panic for his story "The Shunned House" (*CF* 1.458–62).

Vampires were also involved in Lovecraft's personal life—at least to the degree they were the subject of interest of a brief epistolary intruder into his literary circle of friends. G. P. Olson of Sheldon, Iowa, was a fan who persistently bothered Clark Ashton Smith with deranged letters about vampires in 1932, including one in May 1932 where he informed Smith, in the author's words, "He says that there is no death in the first place, and that Christ was a vampire. Also that a vampire is in "reality" an idealist, with an earth-gravity of 50 per cent. Whatever the hell that means" (Derie 91). In an April 1932 letter to Carl Jacobi, Hugh B. Cave wrote that "I believe now that he is a Swede (note his constant references to the Swedish language). He also speaks a mongrel French and Spanish . . . I don't take his spelling to be a sign of ignorance—rather to be a sign of his unfamiliarity with our language" (Derie 95–97).

Lovecraft noted in a letter to Smith that Olson's interest in immortality stemmed from the idea that blood is death, and the route to immortality is therefore to stop eating the food needed to make blood, which is why vampires are immortal (Derie 100).

A "telephone game" emerged as the Lovecraft circle passed around news and letters and copies of Olson's writing throughout 1932—in addition to Smith, Lovecraft, Jacobi, and Cave, Olson's writings and opinions also made it to Derleth, Howard, and Henry S. Whitehead, among others (Derie 99). This game of literary tag mirrors the word-of-mouth campaign that spread news of Tommy and *The Room* in the critical mass period between the film's 2003 release and 2009 emergence from cult film to into pop culture. But the character of Olson himself offers some strange parallels. An immigrant with a hidden past and shaky grasp of English, some knowledge of French, an obsession with immortality, and strange views on food and the flying ability of vampires . . . could Olson be Tommy himself?

This is not the first claim that Tommy may have had a different identity in the past. Aside from Sestero's suspicion that he was the Zodiac Killer, in 2014 comic artist Randall Munroe proposed the enduring theory that Tommy is actually 1971 skyjacker D. B. Cooper (Munroe). And if Olson/Tommy really was a vampire who could fly as a result, would that not explain Cooper's ability to escape from his skyjacking and never be found? Far-fetched, perhaps . . . but impossible? How can we truly know for sure? Regardless of the vampire connection to the real Tommy, the role of vampires in *The Room* itself will be discussed further below, as part of the film's indisputably Lovecraftian plot and themes.

The Lovecraftian The Room

James Feinberg, co-president of Providence's own Brown University Film Forum, identified *The Room* as a work advocating nihilism: "If *The Room* is without purpose, Wiseau seems to be telling us, it is only because life itself is without purpose, and it deserves a cinematic anthem to match." If there is a better description of Lovecraft's cosmicism, especially as a guide for film adaptations, I have yet to encounter it. On the other hand, Feinberg's description of the nihilism evoked by *The Room* seems to be at odds with the existential dread felt by the film's crew when they realized what they had gotten themselves into during filming, and the outright horror felt by viewers when seeing the naked Tommy/Johnny in *The Room*'s multiple sex scenes (*TDA* 167–68). Indeed, some of the crew considered the sight of Johnny to be comparable to the Loch Ness Monster, a creature that Lovecraft also commented on (*TDA* 168; Lovecraft and Smith 543).

Aside from its cosmic dread, on a more basic level the Lovecraftian "genre" is typically described as a mix of science fiction and horror, with extraterrestrials taking the place of the purely supernatural. As mentioned above, both Tommy and Sestero have experience in horror films themselves, and Tommy is interested in both vampires and Tommy's Planet. In the climax of *The Room,* Mark angrily asks Johnny during their confrontation, "What planet are you from?" A few shots later, a distraught Johnny proclaims, "I'm fed up with this world!" In the 2010 video game *The Room Tribute*—fan-made but endorsed by Sestero (*TDA* 196)—the developers take these comments at face value, revealing at the end that Johnny was an undercover alien sent to Earth on a mission for his race (Fulp). Among *The Room*'s cast, Kyle Vogt was an actual employee of NASA's Jet Propulsion Laboratory (JPL) (*TDA* 170). JPL handles most of NASA's unmanned space probes; Caitlín R. Kiernan has suggested that at least some of JPL's probes could have encountered the extraterrestrial entities that Lovecraft wrote about (91–92).

While Johnny being an alien is an extrapolation by fans (if an entirely logical one), Tommy almost did make him a supernatural entity of another sort. In one scene of the film, Tommy considered having Johnny fly his car off a rooftop and into the sky. When pressed by Sestero about the thought process behind such a decision, Tommy's response was, "It's just possible side plot. Maybe Johnny is vampire" (*TDA* 92). While the connection between vampirism and flying cars is novel, it is evocative of the flying Mi-Go of "The Whisperer in Darkness" (*CF* 2.470) or the night-gaunts of *The Dream-*

Quest of Unknown Kadath (*CF* 2.130–31). It should be noted that such hallmarks of vampire lore as Anne Rice's *The Vampire Chronicles* and Joss Whedon's *Buffy the Vampire Slayer* had by this point already established that certain vampires could be classified as Old Ones—certainly fitting for a Lovecraftian pantheon (Rice 219, Whedon).[1]

Beyond the plot elements, there is dialogue in *The Room* that seems to parallel Lovecraft. On the aforementioned prospective car-launching rooftop, Mark muses to Johnny that "People are very strange these days." Perhaps Mark is akin to the psychics at the start of "The Call of Cthulhu" who can sense the arrival of the "strange aeons" predicted by Cthulhu's worshippers (*CF* 2.28, 40). A suspicious Johnny in turn asks Mark, "Do you have some secrets?" in a manner of a typical Lovecraftian protagonist trying in vain to uncover ancient occult knowledge, such as that of the Cthulhu Cult (*CF* 2.24). And when Mark's betrayal ultimately pushes Johnny to suicide, his final words are "God forgive me" —perhaps more in line with the morality imbued upon the Mythos by Tommy's fellow Catholic Derleth.

Certainly, Johnny's suicide, as the result of him unable to handle the secrets of the world around him that he uncovered in the mistaken assumption he could deal with them, is almost stereotypically Lovecraftian. In this, Johnny is perhaps more logical than Danforth, driven insane forever by the obscenity he and Dyer uncovered in Antarctica (*CF* 3.156). And perhaps it is no coincidence either that a DVD of *The Room* itself has been taken to the South Pole by fans, heeding some call from the aether that they themselves may not comprehend (*TDA,* plate 36).

Conclusion

Is this article's attempt to see not only *The Room,* but Tommy Wiseau himself, through a Lovecraftian lens somewhat tongue-in-cheek? To be sure. It is more than a bit of a satire of

---

1. Kristopher Karl Woofter argued (226–36) in a 2019 article that *Buffy the Vampire Slayer* is a pioneering example of Lovecraft's weird fiction genre in TV form.

those who profess ultimate disgust and despair at having to view *The Room*, a parody of those who think only some Lovecraftian terror could have created a person as odd as Tommy. Yet Stephen Walker saw satire and parody as two of Lovecraft's core components (159–61). Any review of *The Room* and of Tommy as a person has to have some element of tongue-in-cheek to it given their own intrinsically over-the-top natures. A Lovecraftian review of the disaster artist and his masterpiece would therefore have to have a parodic element. It is perhaps a softer version of what S. T. Joshi termed satirical criticism, a "fusion of literary criticism—even in the humbling guise of book reviewing—with satire [requiring] something other than insult or abuse" (Joshi, "Satirical Criticism" 98).

But at the same time, I do not believe the connections are entirely without merit, even if Tommy is completely unaware of Lovecraft, and Lovecraft would almost certainly have disliked both *The Room* and Tommy. For all their outlandishness, both *The Room* and Lovecraft's mythos have very sincere cores to them, and central themes of loneliness and alienation—as do both Lovecraft and Tommy. Even if only one of them uses both meanings of "alienation." And in the end, even if I cannot say that Lovecraft would enjoy *The Room*, or that every Lovecraftian aficionado would, the bottom line is that there are far less enjoyable films, and far more which completely miss the themes of Lovecraft, among the various ostensible direct adaptations of his work.

And it is easy enough to imagine some parallel universe where Miskatonic University students are avid members of the college midnight theater circuit, and Tommy and Greg come to host a Q&A showing of *The Room* at Wilmarth Media Hall. What better university at which to show a cult film, after all?

Works Cited

Adomian, James; Scheer, Paul; and Tompkins, Paul F. "Appendix B: Friederich Nietzsche and H. P. Lovecraft, Featuring James Adomian and Paul Scheer." *The Dead Authors Podcast*, 1 May 2012. thedeadauthorspodcast.libsyn.com/

appendix-b-friederich-nietzsche-and-h-p-lovecraft-featuring-james-adomian-and-paul-scheer.

Borowska, Aleksandra. "H. P. Lovecraft's Style in Translation: A Case Study of Selected stories and Their Polish Versions." Ph.D. diss.: Nicolaus Copernicus University in Toruń, 2011.

Clarke, Arthur C. *Astounding Days: A Science Fictional Autobiography*. New York: Bantam, 1990.

Derie, Bobby. "That Fool Olson." *Lovecraft Annual* No. 12 (2018): 90–104.

Feinberg, James. "You're Tearing Me Apart: Tommy Wiseau's *The Room* as Nihilistic Opus." Brown University Film Forum, 27 November 2017. blogs.brown.edu/buff/2017/11/27/youre-tearing-me-apart-tommy-wiseaus-the-room-as-nihilistic-opus/

Fifer, Chad, and Chris Lackey. "Episode 22—The Other Gods." *The H. P. Lovecraft Literary Podcast,* 2 December 2009. hppodcraft.com/2009/12/02/episode-22-the-other-gods/.

Fulp, Tom. *The Room Tribute*. Newgrounds, 2010. www.newgrounds.com/portal/view/547307.

Giovannetti, Nick, and Paul Scheer. *Spider-Man/Deadpool Vol. 1. #12*. New York: Marvel Comics, 2016.

"The Harvest." *Buffy the Vampire Slayer,* Season 1, Episode 2. Created and written by Joss Whedon, directed by John T. Kretchmer. The WB, 1997. [Whedon]

The House That Drips Blood on Alex. Dir. Brock LaBorde and Jared Richard. Atom.com, 2010. Film.

Joshi, S. T. *Lovecraft's Library: A Catalogue*. 3rd ed. New York: Hippocampus Press, 2012.

———. "The Theory and Practice of Satirical Criticism." *Dead Reckonings* No. 23 (Spring 2018): 98–102.

Kiernan, Caitlín R. *Agents of Dreamland*. New York: Tor, 2017.

Lovecraft, H. P. *Collected Essays*. Ed. S. T. Joshi. New York: Hippocampus Press, 2004–06. 5 vols. [*CE*]

———. *Collected Fiction: A Variorum Edition*. Ed. S. T. Joshi. New York: Hippocampus Press, 2015–17. 4 vols. [*CF*]

————. *Selected Letters.* Ed. August Derleth, Donald Wandrei, and James Turner. Sauk City, WI: Arkham House, 1965–76. 5 vols. [*SL*]

————, and Clark Ashton Smith. *Dawnward Spire, Lonely Hill: The Letters of H. P. Lovecraft and Clark Ashton Smith.* Ed. David E. Schultz and S. T. Joshi. New York: Hippocampus Press, 2017.

Munroe, Randall. "D. B. Cooper." *xkcd*, 28 July 2014. xkcd.com/archive/.

Rice, Anne. *The Vampire Lestat.* New York: Ballantine, 1986.

The Room. Dir. Tommy Wiseau. Wiseau-Films, 2003. Film.

Sestero, Greg, and Tom Bissell. *The Disaster Artist: My Life Inside* The Room, *the Greatest Bad Movie Ever Made.* New York: Simon & Schuster, 2013. [*TDA*]

Spaulding, Todd David. "H. P. Lovecraft and the French Connection: Translation, Pulps and Literary History." Ph.D. diss.: University of South Carolina, 2015.

Walker, Stephen. "The Shadow of His Smile: Humor in H. P. Lovecraft's Fiction." In *Lovecraftian Proceedings No. 1: Papers from NecronomiCon Providence 2013,* ed. John Michael Sefel et al. New York: Hippocampus Press, 2015. 151–64.

Woofter, Kristopher Karl. "Weird Whedon: Cosmic Dread and Sublime Alterity in the Whedonverse." In *Joss Whedon vs. the Horror Tradition: The Production of Genre in Buffy and Beyond,* ed. Kristopher Karl Woofter and Lorna Jowett. London: I. B. Tauris, 2019. 219–42.

Weird Fiction in the 21st Century: A Conversation with S. T. Joshi

Alex Houstoun

Having established himself as one of the leading critics of weird fiction in the twentieth century, S. T. Joshi is now looking to document, and dissect, the genre and its writers of the twenty-first century. His recent book, *21st-Century Horror: Weird Fiction at the Turn of the Millennium* (Sarnath Press, 2018), is an exploration of the renaissance of weird writing in recent decades along with sharp analysis of the work of notable authors in the field. In true Joshi fashion, the book is divided into three categories of authors—the "Elite," the "Worthies," and the "Pretenders"—and as generous as he is in his praise for those deemed deserving, *21st-Century Horror* similarly showcases his (in)famous "satirical criticism" in response to those authors and works that he finds to be bloated, hackish messes.

Seemingly not content to take a moment to breathe—in the course of our correspondence, S. T. suggested he is currently juggling at least a half-dozen congruent projects by my count—Joshi was willing to take time over a series of weeks to speak with me via email about *21st-Century Horror,* the simultaneously harsh and liberating financial realities of writing weird fiction, and the current state of criticism in the field.

AH: Here we are, eighteen years into the twenty-first century and we have our first book studying weird fiction in this millennium. It is remarkable! You write in the introduction that there has been an "explosion of weird writing in this new century," which seems to be due in part to the "bewilderingly wide range of what today is regarded as weird fiction." Do you have a theory as to what may have led to this explosion or the broadening concept of what constitutes weird fiction? Are there other factors that have helped contribute to this proliferation in the genre?

STJ: I believe there are a multitude of factors involved in the proliferation of weird fiction over the past few decades. Paradoxically, the end of the horror "boom" of the 1970s and 1980s may have aided in this process, by weeding out many of the hacks and wannabes (who, now that weird writing is no longer commercially viable, have gone into other fields or drifted away from hack writing altogether and gotten honest jobs), leaving the field open for sincere strivers. I also think that the extensive reprinting of the classics of weird fiction (stretching back to Poe, and going on to Ambrose Bierce, Lovecraft, Machen, Dunsany, Blackwood, and many others) allowed contemporary writers to return to the roots of weird writing and also to gain some idea of what kind of fiction had worked in the past. Some of the best weird writing today is an adaptation of classic motifs to present-day circumstances. The proliferation of good writing has led to the expansion of small-press outlets (mostly book publishers rather than magazines), many of whom are doing outstanding work. No one is making a lot of money at the game, but a substantial amount of highly meritorious work is being generated—along, of course, with a certain quantity of rubbish.

AH: I fear this is going to be somewhat obvious, but I am curious if you feel that the Internet has also played a significant role in the current state of weird fiction both as a resource that allows people to discover the classics and also as a way to establish communities in which writers and readers are able to find likeminded people as well as being exposed to new material. In particular, it seems to me that a lot of the success of small-press outlets has had to do with the Internet, as it has made it easier for people to start their own small-press operations and readers to find that material. This book may be a good example of that! You are publishing this book through Sarnath Press, which you describe on your website as a "micro-imprint" that you established to issue some of your writings that you "do not wish to burden other presses with, and also to issue some multi-volume projects . . . that would be impractical to publish by ordinary means." Given the mission statement, it certainly seems that, if not for independent publishing, there may not be an outlet for some of your work.

STJ: Well, yes, the Internet—and computer technology in general—has been a great boon to small-press publishing. That has both its good and bad sides. I am old enough to remember when, in the 1960s and 1970s, small presses in our field were still trying to make do with such primitive reproductive methods as mimeograph or even ditto. The early publications by Necronomicon Press were incredibly crude affairs—the pages reproduced on a photocopy machine (one side of the page only) and stapled at the side. So a magazine or book publisher today can certainly make use of newer technology and produce a handsome-looking project at relatively minimal expense.

That said, the conundrum in the small press (whether in our field or elsewhere) is the simple but monumental issue of financial viability. In other words, how does one make any money by the process, whether it be online sites (which are generally free) or small-press publications on Kindle or other such venues where the price is expected to be extremely low? Even the very few small presses that appear to be financially profitable (e.g., Centipede Press) seem to manage only by producing extremely expensive limited editions. The upshot is that very few people—whether it be authors or editors or publishers—can actually make a living by writing or publishing in the small press. I do so only by sheer quantity production: I have published close to 280 books, very few of which have sold more than a few hundred copies. My Sarnath Press imprint allows me to issue work at literally no cost, since the books are published through Amazon's CreateSpace and Kindle platforms. But, correspondingly, I make relatively little money from them (although I suppose I could make more if I took the trouble to do more advertising and publicity). But the field is not in good shape if many of its major practitioners only do their work as a hobby.

AH: This "simple" issue of financial viability appears to play a large role in *21st-Century Horror*. As you previously noted, weird fiction is no longer the commercially viable genre it was during the horror "boom," and you write in the book's introduction that weird short stories have "never been a marketable commodity." This provides the format with a major benefit: "it allows authors to write pretty much what they wish, without thought of selling their work to a large and indiscriminate audience."

In *21st-Century Horror* you analyze the work of authors as organized in three categories: the "Elites," the "Worthies," and the "Pretenders." Of the "elite" category you acknowledge that it is "no accident" that five of the six authors in the category are "almost entirely devoted to short fiction." In contrast, five of the six authors in your "pretenders" categories are known for novels and that category is generally populated with authors who are probably the most commercially and financially successful of those covered in the book.

Can you explain your process for arranging the book and how you decided upon these three categories? Do you think the difference between the "elites" and the "pretenders" is the preference of short fiction over novels or is it in the difference in writing what one wishes to write versus writing for a large audience?

STJ: My use of the three categories in my book was somewhat *ex post facto*. I started out by simply trying to figure out which authors I should treat in a book of this kind. First, I wished to avoid discussing those authors I had already talked about (even if briefly) in *Unutterable Horror*. (I did make an exception for Laird Barron and Jonathan Thomas, whom I had discussed in that earlier book; they had both done further work that I felt it worth analysing.) Second, I wished to focus on authors whose work appeared predominantly in the twenty-first century rather than earlier (this compelled me to leave out such a writer as Jack Ketchum, who started publishing in the 1980s). Finally, I felt the need to focus on authors who were either intrinsically meritorious (on purely aesthetic grounds) and/or on those who were prominent in the field for one reason or another.

It turned out that a fair number of authors who ended up

being relegated to my "pretenders" category were predominantly novelists; but that may be happenstance. Adam Nevill made the "elite" list, although he is almost entirely known for his novels—and they are, on the whole, commercially successful in the UK. Jonathan Thomas, Gemma Files, and Michael Aronovitz have written at least one novel that is magnificent, although the bulk of their best work is in the short story or novelette. So it certainly can't be said that the mere act of writing novels (even novels consciously written to appeal to a wide audience) necessarily consigns an author to the "pretenders" category. Indeed, several of the writers in that category (Laird Barron, Paul Tremblay, Jeff VanderMeer) appear to have lofty reputations, and my less than flattering assessment of their work was meant to reflect a certain contrarian opinion as to their actual merits.

AH: Speaking of aesthetics, you write that you see "no other viable way to establish literary merit" than turning to "abstract aesthetic considerations," and that the only means of measurement you know of to "winnow out the meritorious from the mediocre" is "pure aesthetic achievement (as opposed to popular appeal or other adventitious traits)."

I recognize that this is a subject you have written about at length in prior works but, for the unfamiliar, can you expound a little on these "considerations" and the particular role they play in assessing a work of weird fiction?

STJ: By purely aesthetic considerations I am referring to basic questions about a text that need to be answered before we can gauge whether it is a meritorious piece of work or not. Does the prose idiom of the work effectively convey the author's message (and I am well aware that there are many ways to write good prose, whether it be the austerity of Hemingway to the lushness of Poe and Lovecraft)? Are the characters vital and vividly portrayed? Is the work's structure compact and efficient, free of extraneous elements (i.e., Poe's "unity of effect")? Most significantly, is the author actually attempting to say something meaningful about human life and its relations to the cosmos, rather than writing a tale merely designed to keep the average reader turning those pages? In the specifically weird realm, is the supernatural component of the work (if there is one) original and not hackneyed, and do all its manifestations in the tale harmonise into a unity rather than being random and incoherent? No doubt there are other such questions, but these will suffice to indicate the *kind* of questions I tend to ask of a text.

For decades there has been a growing tendency in academic criticism (and especially academic scholarship) to shy away from questions of this sort, lest the critic come off as "elitist" or judgmental. And more recently, both academic critics and others seem to value certain other traits in a literary work that strike me as largely adventitious or extraneous; specifically, whether the text conveys a certain sociopolitical orthodoxy. Indeed, much academic criticism now seems entirely focused on questions of race, class, and gender—issues that strike me as more the domain of sociology than of literary criticism.

In effect, this emphasis on aesthetic considerations gets to the very heart of my own critical enterprise. From the beginning of my career as a critic I have attempted to sort the good from the bad, the innovative from the trite, the substantial from the ephemeral. *The Weird Tale* (1990), *The Modern Weird Tale* (2001), and *Unutterable Horror* (2012) were largely written on this premise. I now recognise that this is a central function of criticism. The very word "criticism" is derived from the Greek verb *kritein*—which originally meant "to divide" (e.g., a piece of land), but later developed the meaning of "to distinguish, to discriminate" (e.g., between the meritorious and the mediocre). And I also recognise that this task requires both the vaunting of the meritorious and the exposure of the mediocre. I have stated until I am blue in the face that my judgments are largely suggestive rather than prescriptive; I am always open to contrary opinions, if they are cogently argued.

In *The Modern Weird Tale* I attempted to show that such popular writers as Stephen King, Clive Barker, and Anne Rice were less meritorious than Ramsey Campbell, T. E. D. Klein, Thomas Ligotti, and others. I got a certain amount of blowback from the partisans of the former group, as I expected I would. But that was nothing compared to the tsunami of billingsgate I received when I posted online some of the chapters from the "pretenders" group of *21st-Century Horror*. It would appear that the tribalism so prevalent in today's political sphere now extends even to one's favourite authors. I can understand that sentiment, for in my younger days I regarded any critic's slighting of Lovecraft as a personal insult. But in that case, I did not respond merely with abuse of the given critic but with an exhaustive analysis that sought to demonstrate why I regarded Lovecraft as a worthy and canonical writer. It would appear that my work, and that of my colleagues, has won the day as far as Lovecraft is concerned. But it does not appear that the partisans of Laird Barron or Brian Keene or Jeff VanderMeer are much interested in, or capable of, this kind of critical rigour. And so they descend to the level of Internet trolls.

AH: I recall you joking about how I might react to the "pretenders" section, calling the material "inflammatory," when we were first setting up this interview. While I must admit I disagree with you in some regards—particularly Jeff VanderMeer's Southern Reach trilogy (I am dying to know if you ended up seeing the loose film adaptation)—it is hard not to see your assessment for what you say it is, suggestive rather than prescriptive. You go, I think, to great lengths in *21st-Century Horror* to stress this position and seem to welcome response and rebuttal, writing what you present in the book to be "only an initial, tentative attempt at charting this unruly field, and subsequent studies will no doubt be needed to augment, refine, or refute some of my conclusions."

Having said all that, what I do find challenging, and what caught me off guard when reading the book, is your view that "the intrusion of extraneous sociopolitical considerations" has hamstrung the establishment of a twenty-first-century weird fiction canon. To offer a contrary opinion, and hope I do so in a cogent manner, is it not possible that these considerations are not intrusions but part of an evolution of literary criticism? More so, that they have allowed both critics and readers to ask more of literary works? Not in the sense that critics are demanding that a work meet all the marks on a checklist or convey a "certain sociopolitical orthodoxy," but that critics are recognizing and paying attention to works that are both aesthetically successful but also manage to interrogate sociopolitical norms.

STJ: I think only the chapters on Brian Keene and, to a lesser degree, on Joe Hill and VanderMeer can be said to fit into my model of "satirical criticism," on which I have expatiated in an earlier issue of this journal. But in regard to considerations of race, class, and gender: I think they have a lot to do with the temper of our times, just as past fashions in literary criticism (whether it be the New Criticism of deconstruction or whatever) did. It is certainly a good thing that writers today are giving voice to previously marginalised populations, but I am having trouble determining how this element can somehow be interpreted as affecting the *quality* of a work. Take Gemma Files's novel *Experimental Film* (2015), which I study in my book. It focuses on two female characters—Lois Cairns, a contemporary film critic, and an obscure filmmaker of a century ago, Iris Whitcomb, who may or may not have become a ghost. Both characters are vividly realised; but the merits of the book rest on the originality of its weird conception (having to do with an ancient mythic figure thrust into the present day) and the complex and tightly constructed structure of the novel. Similar assessments can be made in the work of Nicole Cushing, Glen Hirshberg, and others.

AH: Speaking of Nicole Cushing and Glen Hirshberg, you place both authors in the "Worthies" section. This may be a bit tricky, but I wonder if you could elaborate on some of the themes you saw when assembling this part of the book. The authors you feature, I feel, give the reader almost the most generalized sense of the state of contemporary weird fiction in that we have authors who have produced some incredible short stories, less accomplished novels, and, by necessity, seem to publish a decent amount of their work in themed anthologies. More so, these authors seem to play successfully with the very rules or categorization of weird fiction. For example, you write of Cushing, "There may be some question as to whether Cushing actually writes 'weird fiction': relatively little of her work is conventionally supernatural, and much of it ventures into the realms of science fiction, bizarro fiction, metaphysical fables, and tales of psychological terror. Indeed, the bulk of her writing is psychological or philosophical in its essence."

STJ: The distinction between the "elite" and the "worthies" in my book is frankly a bit arbitrary, and I could easily have switched some of them from one category to the other. It is a very tricky thing to attach such labels to authors who are in the midst of their careers; one can never predict what they will do in the coming decades. In some cases—as in those of Cushing and especially Clint Smith—I relegated them to the "worthies" category only because they are still early in their careers and are likely to do even better work in the future. Smith has in fact published only one collection (a second is forthcoming from Hippocampus Press) and a novella. I am not saying that quantity counts for a great deal, but it counts for *something*. A substantial quantity of consistently high output (Ramsey Campbell is, far and away, the best example of this—to such a degree that he may be the greatest writer in the entire history of weird fiction) is an impressive achievement, and I expect several of the "worthies" (and also the "elite") to deliver on this in the years to come.

I should also mention that there are probably other writers, whom I did not cover at all, who are certainly worth discussion. My time for reading newer work is limited by the fact that much of my time is devoted to the editing and analysis of older writing—the work of Lovecraft, Clark Ashton Smith, Lord Dunsany, Ambrose Bierce, and other such writers. I read very slowly; it took me the better part of three years to read enough of the authors I covered in this book to write adequately about them; and in almost no instance could I read *everything* they had written. And there are no doubt other writers who are developing good reputations, but whom I simply did not have the energy to hunt up and analyse. This is why a book of this sort is provisional, in many senses of the term.

AH: You have written both in *Dead Reckonings* and elsewhere about your view of the role of the literary critic and the general need for intelligent criticism. In reading *21st-Century Horror* I couldn't help but wonder if you had any thoughts on the state of weird fiction criticism or if such a thing exists. Are there contemporary critics whom you follow, who are maybe shaping or influencing some aspect of the current era of weird fiction? Or, as I personally fear, are critics being somewhat cast aside as there are increasingly fewer and fewer platforms and publications for a newer critic to develop an audience, let alone an influence?

STJ: I have to confess that in much of my recent criticism I have actually read very little critical work on the books or authors I choose to discuss; this even applies to works such as *Unutterable Horror,* where I relied largely on my own accumulated knowledge of weird fiction and its practitioners over the past two centuries. Perhaps there is a bit of laziness in this, but in the case of the authors I cover in this book there is obviously not a great deal of formal criticism—even in the form of book reviews—available. The book review—especially the extended or detailed book review of the sort that is included in this magazine—appears to be a dying art, chiefly because the venues for them have withered away. When the first version of my biography, *H. P. Lovecraft: A Life* (1996), appeared, it was reviewed in nearly twenty different print venues, ranging from *Necrofile* to *Deathrealm* to *Science-Fiction Studies* to the *New York Review of Science Fiction* to the *SFRA Review*. And this was a book published by a small press. "Reader reviews" of the sort we now find on Amazon are no substitutes. In contrast to the old adage, everyone is *not* a critic; very few have either the wide reading in the given field or (more importantly) the critical judgment to make an informed evaluation of a literary work. I suppose I could have gotten some further insights on the authors I discuss from reading interviews of them; but I wished to focus on their work rather than on their personalities. I do hope there will be continuing forums for criticism in our field; my *Weird Fiction Review* is one (although I am now retired as editor, as the publisher will now use a rotating series of guest editors), and I may establish another journal of that sort in the future.

AH: With regard to the future, you describe the nineteen authors discussed in *21st-Century Horror* as "representative of certain dominant trends in the field over the past several decades." Are there particular trends that you are ready to see retired or abandoned as we continue into the century? On the flip side, are there any emerging themes that you have noticed and are watching or curious to see how they develop?

STJ: I confess that I haven't the slightest idea what are the dominant trends in weird fiction right now. I really don't read enough contemporary fiction to have a valid opinion on this subject. Of course, in the narrow realm of Lovecraftian fiction, I do see writers increasingly drawing upon the fundamental essence of Lovecraft's work—whether it be cosmic alienation or topographical horror or psychic transference—rather than the superficial externals of his tales (the "gods," forbidden books, and the like). I just assembled an interesting volume of stories in which contemporary authors used Lovecraft himself (or a Lovecraft-like figure) as a central character. So much information is now available about Lovecraft that he has become (to my own dumbfoundment) an icon of popular culture. But as for general weird fiction, I'm largely clueless. I certainly hope the dreary popularity of vampires, zombies, and the like is a thing of the past; there is surely little more that can be squeezed out of these stale elements. I think a fair number of writers have done well in incorporating some motifs of classic writers (Machen, Blackwood, M. R. James, and so on) into work that remains vital and contemporary. I think much more could be done along these lines.

AH: So, having now tackled horror in the twenty-first century, what is next? Can you say a little more about this Lovecraftian volume and other projects you might be working on?

STJ: I seem to be unusually busy these days, as I keep taking up new projects or having projects dumped on me. As Lovecraft once said, "More work for an old man!" My anthology about Lovecraft as a character is called *His Own Most Fantastic Creation* (using the felicitous comment by Vincent Starrett that Lovecraft was "his own most fantastic creation") and should be out next year from PS Publishing. PS has been a bit slow in getting out an anthology I completed in 2017, *Apostles of the Weird,* a volume of all-original stories wherein I try to display the wide scope and parameters of weird fiction. But most of my time at the moment is taken up in editing letters—by Lovecraft, Clark Ashton Smith, and others. There is an extraordinary storehouse of information in such documents, and they should lay the groundwork for more detailed and probing analyses of their authors' life and work. I have also just assembled a three-volume edition of Arthur Machen's collected fiction. But I do take up less weighty projects from time to time. I have just completed a short detective novel, *Honeymoon in Jail,* featuring Lovecraft and his wife Sonia as detectives! It's pure frivolity, but I like to think the core mystery element is decently handled. So it's not all work and no play for me!

AH: In prior interviews I have tried to end by asking the interviewee what they are currently reading. While I am very curious what you may be currently reading, I was also curious if you would also be willing to share some of the authors who you may have liked to include in *21st-Century Horror* but didn't due to various restraints.

Basically, who are you currently reading for your own pleasure and, if one is an incredibly ambitious reader looking for suggestions beyond those made in *21st-Century Horror*, what would be your recommendations?

STJ: After finishing my reading for *21st-Century Horror,* I decided to take a break from horror and have been happily reading detective stories (mostly from the 1930s and 1940s) as a way of relaxing my mind. But there are so many good or up-and-coming authors in the weird field that I can do little but list a few of them: Tom Fletcher, Curtis M. Lawson, Mike Allen, Michael Griffin, Livia Llewellyn, etc. etc. And let's not forget some very fine weird poets, such as Ann K. Schwader,

Wade German, Leigh Blackmore, Benjamin Blake, D. L. Myers, Christina Sng, and many others. A whole treatise needs to be written on weird poetry—and perhaps I may get to that someday.

AH: Well, we will have to do this again should that treatise come to pass! Thank you very much for taking the time to talk with me.

Rediscovering Ken Greenhall

Darrell Schweitzer

KEN GREENHALL. *Elizabeth*. Richmond, VA: Valancourt
Books 2017. 152 pp. $14.99 tpb. ISBN: 978-1-943910-67-0.
KEN GREENHALL. *Hell Hound*. Richmond, VA: Valancourt Books 2017. 139 pp. $14.99 tpb. ISBN: 978-1-
943910-65-6.
KEN GREENHALL. *Childgrave*. Richmond, VA: Valancourt Books 2017. 275 pp. $16.99 tpb. ISBN: 978-1-
943910-87-8.

Surely the greatest service any critic can render to the reading
public is to bring about the revival of worthy but forgotten
work. Kudos are due to Grady Hendrix, whose enormously
entertaining *Paperbacks from Hell* (2017) not only wittily sur-
veys the vast flood of strange and often quite trashy paperback
original horror novels of the Boom Years (circa 1968–94) but
reassures us that, yes, some of them actually were good.

His major discovery was Ken Greenhall, and this should be
acknowledged as a discovery rather than a *re*discovery, because, to be candid, Greenhall was never previously known.
As someone who was active in the horror field, publishing
professionally, interviewing authors, reviewing books, and at-
tending conventions during the period in question, I can tell
you that I never heard the name. Credit is certainly due to the
editors of the time perceptive enough to accept and publish
Greenhall's material, but, alas, the publishers brought these
books out as throwaways, with covers that virtually guaranteed that no one would take them seriously. Sure enough,
Greenhall's work got swept along and away with the flood of
other cheapie horror novels that were impossible to keep track
of, even then.

Elizabeth, his first, was published under the byline of Jessica Hamilton (the author's mother's maiden name) by Popular
Library in 1976. That the byline never appeared again certain-

ly helped the book's quick drop into oblivion. In brief, nobody noticed. It was not until 2017 that Hendrix pointed out how sublimely good this novel actually is. I will not go so far as to claim it is an equal to *The Haunting of Hill House,* but it does point in that direction. *Elizabeth* is a novel of witchcraft, narrated by a sociopathic fourteen-year-old girl, and it might be loosely described as what would have resulted if Shirley Jackson had written *Lolita.* The title character is strangely mature for her age, but, as we begin to realize, she is completely without compassion. She is already in a sexual relationship with her uncle by the time we meet her, but she does not see herself as a victim. She is looking to exploit it, as a way of manipulating her uncle. Then she encounters her own ancestor Frances, a sixteenth-century witch who appears to her in mirrors. Before long, Elizabeth has a familiar, and has performed a sinister little rite that very likely caused the deaths of her parents. She admits as much, although when she does something similar to make her grandmother disappear, she is for some time uncertain of what precisely happened, and whether she, or someone else, actually killed the grandmother.

The question the book doesn't quite come to terms with is whether Elizabeth is inherently evil—the bad seed of a family of witches—or whether she has chosen to be this way. In any case, *Elizabeth* is masterfully understated, and a fine, chilling novel, and it would have been a memorable debut, if anyone had noticed at the time.

This was followed in 1977 by *Hell Hound,* published under Greenhall's own name, but again, as disposable trash by Zebra Books with an appalling cover guaranteed to make sure the book would be lost among the killer voles, rabbits, bats, crabs, or whatever that were infesting paperback shelves about then.

This time the protagonist is a strangely articulate, psychopathic *dog.* Not an anthropomorphized animal. It does not talk. It behaves like a dog. But it thinks, and narrates some sections of the book. Baxter, the dog, is *not* man's best friend, but looking out for Number One always, and not at all hesitant about pushing an old lady down a flight of stairs or drowning a baby if this will result in a more agreeable "master" and better living circumstances. For much of the story he seems ideally matched with Carl, age twelve, a wannabe Nazi and precocious in his depravity. But things don't quite work out as planned, and the most chilling note struck at the end is the suggestion that Carl has gained in evil, not so much from the example of Hitler, but from Baxter. This is a weird book by any standard, briskly paced and powerful. It was even filmed in France, as *Baxter* (1989), directed by Jerome Boivin. The film was featured by John Waters as an episode of *John Waters Presents Movies That Will Corrupt You*. So will the book corrupt you perhaps, but both remain surprisingly little-known.

In *Childgrave*, published by Pocket Books in 1982, Greenhall was obviously flexing his auctorial muscles. His third novel is twice as long as either of his first two. In some ways it is less successful, as it begins as a rather slow-paced romantic comedy that only gradually becomes spooky as the photographer protagonist becomes involved with a mysterious woman who seems to be able to generate ghost-images on film. Ultimately there is a strange town with an effectively hideous, centuries-old secret, but it takes us some time getting there. Before that, *Childgrave* reads like a slightly off-kilter Jonathan Carroll novel about brilliant, artistic people living upper-class New York lives, into which strangeness slowly creeps. Greenhall even has Carroll's knack for snappy narrative hooks:

> There was a time when my life was like yours. I ate veal occasionally and avoided people who had a serious interest in God. I smiled at clients during the day, disappearing beneath the black velvet hood from time to time to steal their souls.

After this, Grady Hendrix tells us, Greenhall published two more horror novels, *The Companion* (1988) and *Deathchain* (1991), which he implies are not as good as the first three. Valancourt has not reprinted them. Then Greenhall's agent disappeared and he was unable to get further representation, often being told he was "too old." He was all of sixty-three in 1991, but there is indeed age discrimination in publishing, as publishers do not so much buy individual books as invest in the upward curve of a writer's career. Greenhall, at that age, with five apparently cheapie generic novels behind him, must not have looked like a promising investment. It is a hard fact that commercial publishing works this way. It is a harder one that these decisions are often made by people who have not read any of the books in question. Despite this, Greenhall was able to sell one more novel, one that he had been contemplating for years. It wasn't generic, or even horror. It was *Lenoir* (1998), a historical novel about the seventeenth-century black man who posed for Rubens's *Four Studies of the Head of a Negro*. It was published by an obscure house, Zoland Books. I haven't read it, although I intend to and have a copy. (Since it is still unknown, it can be found quite cheaply on eBay.) Hendrix says it is very good. It got some favorable reviews when it came out, then was condescendingly panned in the *New York Times*. Greenhall was apparently so discouraged that he never wrote again. He died in 2014.

A tragic tale of neglect, of an all too common sort. The good news is that some of his work has been reprinted. The conclusion I draw is that even if Greenhall's books are not quite sublime masterpieces to go ringing down the ages, they are good, considerably better than much of what was published during horror's boom years, and they deserve further attention. There is another lesson here, too, that has nothing to do with literary quality, but everything to do with how to conduct a career. It is useful for a writer to socialize and network. Perhaps Thomas Pynchon and J. D. Salinger could become famous as mysterious recluses, but most writers who try that road will end up like Ken Greenhall. If he had been a regular at Stoker Cons and World Fantasy and NECon, if he had been a familiar panelist and pal of other writers, I am sure his career would have turned out differently. Someone would have found him another agent. He almost certainly would have discovered, or been discovered by the horror specialty presses. Someone like Scream/Press or Dark Regions might have done fancy hardcover reprints of his novels for the collector market. He might have been encouraged to write short fiction for *Cemetery Dance* and *Shadows*.

Instead, alas, we never heard his name when he was alive, and are only discovering him now.

Some Notes on *Call of Cthulhu* and Other Lovecraftian Video Games

Géza A. G. Reilly

Call of Cthulhu: The Official Video Game. Cyanide Studio. Focus Home Interactive, 2018. $44.99, Microsoft Windows, PlayStation 4 and Xbox One.

It would be an understatement to describe the anticipation for *Call of Cthulhu*'s October 30, 2018 release as anything less than profound. The game had gone through an extended and intense development cycle after being announced almost four years prior, and fans of Lovecraft and the horror genre alike were eager to see what could be done with a property that had the official stamp of approval from Chaosium, Inc., the publishers of the *Call of Cthulhu* pen-and-paper role-playing game. However, the Metacritic scores (67 out of 100 for critics and 7 out of 10 for users) suggest that the game has not accomplished all that it set out to do. Generally speaking, a video game (even one from a mid-range developer like Cyanide Studios) that receives a passing 'D' or gentleman's 'C' grade is considered to be the worst thing, perhaps, that a piece of media can be: unremarkable with some bad, but not catastrophic, elements. Was *Call of Cthulhu*, then, an ambitious game released to an unappreciative market? Or is there a deeper reason for its lack of ability at standing out?

The history of Lovecraftian video games is one fraught with disappointment. For every *Anchorhead* (Michael Gentry, 1998) or *Eternal Darkness: Sanity's Requiem* (Silicon Knights, 2002), it seems as though there are a baker's dozen titles that fall short of making an impact within the weird fiction community. The reason for this seems to be an evergreen bone of contention among Lovecraft and horror fiction fans. Is there a difference between Lovecraftian fiction (that is, fiction evocative of the work of H. P. Lovecraft himself) and Cthulhu Mythos fiction (that is, pastiches that hinge on the trappings used in Lovecraft's writing)? I am hesitant to give a definitive opinion on the matter here, but I think it is safe to say that many people take issue with the fact that so many purportedly Lovecraftian video games are, for lack of a better term, *Cthulhu Mythos* video games in actuality.

That is, the vast majority of Lovecraftian video games fail to capture the frisson of a Lovecraft story because they put their narrative focus on the trappings of the Mythos without *using* those trappings to say something of substance beyond giving the player an enjoyable narrative experience. In some respects, debates about horror video games centering on whether or not a given game is actually *scary* tie into the Lovecraftian/Cthulhu Mythos divide. Being frightening is certainly an element of narrative design that is important and is sadly lacking from all too many Lovecraftian video games. However, I think that it is much more important, on an analytic level, to consider whether a video game has something important to say above and beyond merely being frightening. *Silent Hill 2* (Konami, 2001), for example, is a horror game that, while not necessarily frightening to some players, is widely regarded as having something important to say about guilt, loss, and psychological obsession (and it is, perhaps not coincidentally, widely considered a pseudo-Lovecraftian game due to its atmosphere and design despite not using *any* of the window dressing of the Mythos).

So where does *Call of Cthulhu* fall in terms of these divides? Is *Call of Cthulhu* frightening? In parts, yes, though of course it would be impossible to say that such a subjective experience will be enjoyed by all players. Perhaps more importantly, though, is this: does *Call of Cthulhu* have anything to say above and beyond its frightening aspects? Sadly, I think the answer to that is a resounding no. *Call of Cthulhu* has all the window dressing one could want, and thus it most certainly is a Cthulhu Mythos narrative, but it does not have any of the depth, staying power, or wide-ranging narrative ambition that a Lovecraftian game should.

This is not to say that *Call of Cthulhu* is a bad game. In terms of gameplay, artistic design, voice acting, and even plot, the game is an enjoyable experience. The character of Edward

Pierce, the protagonist, is well constructed, and his exploration of the foreboding Darkwater Island in an attempt to discover the fate of the Hawkins family means traveling through atmospheric locations rich in period aesthetics. And yet, now that almost half a year has gone by since I first beat *Call of Cthulhu*, I find that the game made almost no impact on my memory. Surely it is no problem for a piece of media to have about as much impact as a carnival ride, but it does not say much for that media in terms of its success as a work of art.

And video games, Lovecraftian and otherwise, are capable of rising to that level. It may be the rare video game that can be safely counted as art (see the aforementioned *Silent Hill 2* for an example), but surely the same could be said for any given medium. Some films, for example, will disappear into the maw of oblivion over the decades, but some will be remembered as high watermarks in their medium's history of the production of art. *Call of Cthulhu* will not, I think, be so remembered, but that is fine. We all need carnival rides now and again even if they do not stay with us for long.

Thankfully, while the ride that is *Call of Cthulhu* lasts, it is an enjoyable one. The player controls Edward Pierce, a detective, who is hired by the father of famed artist Sarah Hawkins to go to her home on Darkwater Island (a dismal, disenfranchised place off the coast of Boston) to investigate the deaths of her and her family. Being almost entirely free of combat, the first-person game relies almost exclusively on Pierce's skills (updated by experience points earned by completing tasks) to navigate puzzles, interact with the inhabitants of Darkwater, and generally piece together the mystery surrounding the island itself. Any player of the *Call of Cthulhu* RPG will immediately recognize the game systems that the *Call of Cthulhu* video game uses, but those unfamiliar with the tabletop version of the game should not fret: barring one or two opaque moments (such as the game not telling you at character creation that the occultism and medical skills cannot be improved by spending experience later in the game), the systems are generally intuitive and simple to master.

The world that those systems support is well built and populated. Each environment is striking in its own way, and both beauty and disgust abound in Edward's exploration of those environments. The characters that Edward meets on his journey are generally well written and acted, and they suggest an extensive history of the island and its inhabitants that gives an interesting depth to the otherwise linear plot. While that plot is, as said, ultimately forgettable, I did enjoy it while playing the game—and, in fact, some moments made me sit forward in my chair, enthralled briefly by a bit of clever writing or stylish delivery. The systems and plot do dovetail together in a way that allows for significant replayability; though I myself have not yet gone back through the game, there are different methods of exploration, interpersonal dialogue, and character shaping that lead to attaining one of four (or possibly five; the player base is rather torn on the exact number) distinctly different endings.

Is *Call of Cthulhu* worth playing? Yes, inasmuch as it is an enjoyable romp through the Cthulhu Mythos and many of its associated trappings laid out like pieces on a chessboard. Is it particularly memorable? No, I do not think so, and thus I would not recommend purchasing it without a discount. Is it the Lovecraftian game that many of us in the weird fiction community have been waiting for? No, sadly not. *Call of Cthulhu* is an enjoyable adventure worthy of its tabletop RPG ancestor, but ultimately it has nothing to say other than to remind us of the fact that this particular artistic medium has, as yet, largely remained unexplored in terms of its Lovecraftian potential. *Call of Cthulhu* is currently available for purchase on the PS4 and XBox One consoles and on PC through the Steam platform.

Running toward Nothing:
B. Catling's Vorrh Trilogy

Daniel Pietersen

B. CATLING. *The Vorrh*. New York: Vintage, 2015. 512 pp. $16.99 tpb. ISBN: 978-1-1018-7378-6.
B. CATLING. *The Erstwhile*. New York: Vintage, 2017. 480 pp. $16.99 tpb. ISBN: 978-1-1019-7272-4.
B. CATLING. *The Cloven*. New York: Vintage, 2018. 448 pp. $16.99 tpb. ISBN: 978-1-1019-7274-8.

The strange thing about forests is that they don't really exist. Or, to put it another way, forests only exist when viewed as forests. A forest is a collection of trees and the myriad plants that fill the gaps between trees, the glades and pathways that perforate the density of plant matter, the animals and humans who might live within it. If a tree falls or an animal dies, then you will still have a forest because the forest exists as an idea outside of its constituent parts—ill-defined and nebulous but resilient.

Yet we know a forest when we see one. In many ways, we are pre-programmed to see forests—to see collections of small constituents as gestalt wholes—rather than become lost in the fractal detail of the world. As soon as we can, we elevate our understanding from one level of detail to the next. We say that someone "can't see the wood for the trees" when they become bogged down in detail and pedantry. If a tree falls in a forest and nobody is there to acknowledge it, does it matter? No, because the forest remains and it is the forest, not the tree, that matters.

So you ask: what does all this have to do with reviewing a book? It is a warning, in a roundabout way, that your allegories may turn against you.

The Vorrh is a story about forests. A forest, specifically; the Vorrh being the name of the angel- and demon-haunted forest that lurks at the center of the narrative both figuratively and literally. Yet it is also a story about constituents and gestalts, as evidenced not only by the fact that *The Vorrh* is the first installment in the Vorrh trilogy but by Catling's blending of real and imaginary characters into the narrative. It tells the tale of how humans and angels, known as Rumours and The Erstwhile in the series argot, are each attempting to recover something they have lost and, in finding it, lose even more.

The main joy in this series is to explore its density, so I'm not going to dwell too heavily on major plot points or provide a narrative overview in this review. You can find your own path through this particular forest and you will no doubt find a different path from the one I took. What I will do is stand back, quite far back, and look at the forest that the book creates. When I speak of "The Vorrh" from now on I am referring to the trilogy as a whole.

Brian Catling is, above all, a poet and the language used to construct The Vorrh is rarely less than dizzyingly poetic, almost Gormenghastian, in its arcane manufacture. Lyrical vignettes sparkle like waterfalls in some sunlit glade, and even the most vile scenes—flesh is persistently broken and debased while half-human creatures writhe in agony under peaty soils—have a kind of sublime beauty that makes them feel more unknowable than unpleasant. When Catling talks about Cyrena's blindness, for example, or Meta's fist-clenched fury, these characters jump into sharp relief and seem to glow on the page. The weirdly labyrinthine city of Essenwald also bends and mutates as Catling decides to describe first this section and then another—first Teutonic cobbles and then Moorish carpeting.

The reader is drawn along, flicking between times and characters and narratives and realities to . . .

Well, that's entirely the problem. To where indeed?

Brian Catling is, above all, a poet. He is not, despite the amount of words used to write The Vorrh, an author.

After a while—not actually that long a while—it becomes fairly obvious that the dense and deft language is a cover for a very thin and ill-considered plot. If indeed there is a plot at all.

Things happen, but for no apparent reason, and each book just seems to end until the whole trilogy, in its own way, just ends. What at first I thought was a lack of drive is revealed as an excess of drive. Narrative threads are either forgotten or left to dangle as Catling skitters to the next object of his interests, of which he has many. In fact, Catling flicks from character to theme so quickly and so superficially that the experience of The Vorrh becomes very much like reading a Boy's Own adventure as random Wikipedia entries are mansplained at you.

Eadweard Muybridge, who is working on a consciousness-expanding zoopraxiscope at the behest of (obviously) Sir William Gull—explaining, in one fell swoop, Alan Moore's gushing praise for at least the first volume of The Vorrh trilogy—travels to meet rifle heiress Sarah Winchester at her ever more labyrinthine and ever more haunted house, ostensibly to try and photograph evidence of the hauntings. After much long-winded discussion and extemporizing this whole digression is dismissed *by Muybridge himself* as a waste of time and is never mentioned again, nor does it have any real impact on Muybridge or the wider story.

One of the Erstwhile—who was (again, obviously) the inspiration for William Blake's Nebuchadnezzar—has renamed himself Nicholas Parson, a name he appears to have heard on the radio even though the story is set when the real Nicholas Parsons was only one year old, apparently purely so that Catling can indulge in some Just A Minute-esque whimsy.

The Bakelite faux-robots that tend to Ishmael and lurk menacingly in a basement for reasons that are never completely explained are named after the children of Adam and Eve, do you see, because that's suitably angelic (even though they appear to have no connection to the Erstwhile).

Add all that to characters simply falling off cliffs when they're no longer needed, the Vorrh's memory-eroding ability only really working when it needs to, mysterious voices and note-deliverers remaining mysterious when it is realized we won't meet them again, one of the key character's CORK-SCREW PIG PENIS suddenly not being a weird thing—and the whole forest, albeit constructed from sturdy trees, starts to feel very patchy indeed.

And once you realize how patchy The Vorrh actually is, that's when you realize it also starts to become pretty sketchy.

Beyond the problems that The Vorrh has with its narrative and construction it is also very Capital-P Problematic. The whole mansplaining, do-you-see-how-clever-I-am tone of the books is only a symptom of how very, very white middle-class male they are (that the pull-quote praise lavished on the book is also all from white middle-class males should, in hindsight, have been a premonition of this).

Female characters become hysterical and broody (or maliciously contrary) whenever a jolt of conflict is needed, their interactions with one another often feeling clockwork and insubstantial. Homosexuality is dealt with in an innuendo-laden way that never lets anyone less than lustfully heterosexual seem fully formed. Characters of color are treated even worse as they stroll out, with their rolling eyes and jangling fetishes, of the most frenzied excesses of colonial fever dreams.

Which is ironic because, as much as The Vorrh wants to be a story about rebellion and defiance, it is a hugely colonial narrative, in the deepest and most imperialist senses of that word. Native civilization and belief, even nature itself, is persistently shown as unreliable and malevolent. This could well be meant to indicate the Western characters' views, but it feels so pervasive and ingrained through the narrative that it seems a far deeper concern. Equally, the dominance of white male characters is inescapable; Muybridge's device 'elevates' an African woman to furious enlightenment, Williams creates a magical bow from the body of his native wife (who, again, is defined almost entirely by her mystical and unknowable nature), and native workers in the Vorrh are reduced to leering, insensate animals who have an inexplicable appetite for aborted fetuses. Admittedly, the colonial figures themselves aren't shown in a particularly ingratiating light (nobody is, in many ways, which adds to the tiresomeness of the series), but they still have power and position to add agency to their unpleasantness.

Ultimately, I found The Vorrh to be a frustrating and tedious read, with the poetic prose being stretched increasingly thin to disguise ever deeper shortcomings as it rumbled on to its anticlimactic finale. Worse, perhaps, even than that is the fact that the story doesn't actually say anything of any real interest or insight over three books (and there is absolutely no need for this to be three books). Catling no doubt thinks of the books as a rumination on the human condition—beast, man, and angel simultaneously—when it is really an Ozymandian memorial to boorishness and stolidity.

If The Vorrh is any kind of forest, then it is one daubed on a theater backdrop, seemingly lush and exotic from the stalls but truly little more than stained canvas supported by aged and worm-ridden plywood.

The Horror of Mendacity

Acep Hale

DANIEL POWELL. *Horror Culture in the New Millennium: Digital Dissonance and Technohorror.* Lanham, MD: Lexington, 2019. 168 pp. $90 hc. ISBN 978-1-4985-8744-0. $85 ebook. ISBN 978-1-4985-8745-7.

There has been a resurgence, as of late, in delving horror's depths for philosophical content. This renewed academic exploration is part of a recurring cycle. Previously, in the early '90s, Carol J. Clover published her seminal work *Men, Women, and Chain Saws: Gender in the Modern Horror Film,* which was so influential it crossed over into public consciousness to introduce the concept of the "final girl." Clover turned contemporary thinking of slasher films on its head, throwing then-current ideas of gender roles within horror films into confusion as men within these works were hunted and killed, requiring the final girl to "man up" in order to defeat their stalkers.

Concurrently the student-run collective CCRU (Cybernetic Culture Research Unit) at the University of Warwick's philosophy department, under the guidance of Sadie Plant and Nick Land, mined the works of H. P. Lovecraft for their concepts of hyperstition, results of which strongly influenced the fields now referred to as accelerationism, object-oriented ontology, and speculative realism. The influence of CCRU has been felt strongly in the works of Mark Fisher (*The Weird and The Eerie,* 2017), Graham Harman (*Weird Realism: Lovecraft and Philosophy,* 2012; *Speculative Realism: An Introduction,* 2018), Reza Negarestani (*Cyclonopedia,* 2008), Amy Ireland (*Aesthetics After Finitude,* 2016; "Noise: An Ontology of the Avant-Garde," 2016), and Eugene Thacker's "Horror of Philosophy" trilogy (*In the Dust of This Planet,* 2011; *Starry Speculative Corpse,* 2015; *Tentacles Longer Than Night,* 2015). Thacker's work, particularly *In the Dust of This Planet,* repeated Clover's accomplishment of two decades previous in crossing over into public consciousness when the cover of the book was prominently featured in Jay-Z and Beyonce's "On the Run" video, covered in an episode of NPR's *Radiolab,* worked its way into the script of *True Detective,* and was denounced by Glenn Beck.

In a similar vein Kier-La Janisse's *House of Psychotic Women* has been universally hailed by both readers and critics alike for its "confessional/critical" mode of exploring our fascination with viewing the horrific. Unsatisfied, as most aficionados of the genre are, with the pat explanation that horror allows its viewers to exorcise their own fears in a safe environment, Janisse embarked upon an in-depth exploration of her own relationship with the horror and exploitation genres while chronicling in unflinching detail traumatic events from her own history as they entangled with the films she was viewing. This new mode of criticism, interweaving scholarly deconstruction with stark, emotional honesty, struck chords so deeply that when I attended the Dublin Ghost Story Festival last June I met three women who were completing their Ph.D.s in Literary or Film Studies of horror that all cited *House of Psychotic Women* as a key factor in their decision to pursue their advanced degrees. This is not an isolated incidence. While involved in events put on by the Morbid Anatomy Museum here in New York City Janisse's book was frequently a touchstone either in guest presentations or mentioned in conversations following such. Fittingly, Janisse is the film programmer for the Alamo Draft House and founder of the Miskatonic Institute of Horror Studies.

The thread that binds these works, and others such as Tania Modleski's *The Women Who Knew Too Much: Hitchcock and Feminist Theory,* Barry Keith Grant's *The Dread of Difference,* and Kevin Wetmore Jr.'s *Post-9/11 Horror in American Cinema,* to name just a worthy few, may best be summed up by Alan Moore in his seminal essay, "Writing for Comics," published in 1985:

> Changing the trappings of the comic industry isn't enough. New printing techniques, new characters, new computer

graphic facilities . . . none of these will make the slightest scrap of difference unless the fundamental assumptions upon which the artform itself rests are challenged and modified to fit the times for which they were not originally designed . . . The reason why comic writing is perhaps even a greater cause for concern than comic book drawing is that writing comes at the very start of the process. If the thinking behind the writing is inadequate, the script is inadequate.

Unfortunately, I doubt Daniel Powell's *Horror Culture in the New Millennium: Digital Dissonance and Technohorror* will be joining in this conversation. I had high hopes for the volume going in, as I truly love writings on the subject of horror and believe this is an area that would benefit from deeper exploration, yet I feel the work in question is probably best used as an exhibition piece for the perils of academic publishing in the twenty-first century.

This volume feels from start to finish as if it suffers from the dual problem of an academic under the threat of "publish or perish" while pursuing the economic reward of writing a textbook that will be a mandatory purchase for future students. Given the exorbitant price of this work versus the content within, especially compared to the works cited previously and the publishing house of the volume, this is not an impertinent question. One must ask, in the year 2019, who needs be surprised at the rise in popularity of ebook reading? Or Reddit? Kickstarter? Yet Powell has an entire chapter devoted to "Pioneering Platforms" that will surely be out of date by the second year this book is used in any course, requiring it to be "updated and expanded," and of course used copies that could formerly be purchased at the university bookstore will be rendered useless. A cunning move on the part of the author and/or publisher, but in an environment where textbook prices have risen 1000% since the 1980s not one to buttress support among anyone else.

As for an in-depth exploration of how advancements in technology have changed the production of works of horror, I find Jeff VanderMeer's essay "City of Saints and Madmen: The Untold Story" (2004) to contain far more clarity and insight than anything within Powell's book. The essay is freely available to anyone with a web browser and an Internet connection and, at fifteen years old, manages to be more relevant and to speak to contemporary conditions better than *Horror Culture in the New Millennium.*

Which brings us to another damning point: this book looks worse than a Print-on-Demand book produced in 2004. I know this because I own a copy of VanderMeer's *City of Saints and Madmen* from that time and it stands head and shoulders above the print quality of *Horror Culture.* As one example, the chart on page nine, "Taxonomy of The Horrific," is so low-resolution that it reminds one of looking through the test lenses at the optometrist. In an age and genre that gives us stunning works produced by publishers such as Tartarus, Centipede Press, Zagava, and Hippocampus Press, all at smaller print runs and significantly lower price points than the work in question, this is simply unacceptable. If this book existed in the open marketplace it would be quickly remaindered for one-eighth its current asking price, and even then there would be a long line of works that would take precedence for your purchasing dollar.

From the very beginning of *Horror Culture,* you feel as if you are wading through regurgitated thought. At this point I sincerely doubt that anyone remotely interested in this subject area needs Freud's theory of the Uncanny repeated. However, three pages in, there it is, staring the reader in the face. As Alan Moore noted, if the thinking behind the writing is inadequate. . . . More interesting is the point raised by J. F. Martel, author of *Reclaiming Art in the Age of Artifice* and co-host of the *Weird Studies* podcast, wherein he stated that he has been reading Freud as a weird fiction writer himself, for no one, except Freud and possibly Thomas Ligotti, has ever looked at a doll or puppet and questioned whether they themselves were an inanimate object. Which is not to say Freud has no relevance on the topic, as writers such as Julie Kristeva have proven repeatedly with works such as *Powers of Horror: An Essay on Abjection,* yet to quote Alan Moore once again, "none of these will make the slightest scrap of difference unless the fundamental assumptions upon which the artform itself rests are challenged and modified to fit the times for which they were not originally designed." Powell instead recycles the same talking points that now cause reader's eyes to gloss over at the mention of the *unheimlich,* doing scant personal work to add insight or clarity that will add frisson to the reader's experience.

I realize it is received wisdom while writing reviews that one is supposed to say something nice with each critical point that is raised, yet with *Horror Culture in the New Millennium* I'm going to give that advice a hard pass. This book has the insight of a Medium article, the passion of a PowerPoint presentation, and the integrity of a MultiLevel Marketing meeting. It would not exist without a forced audience that it is pitilessly gouging, and even then I wouldn't lay Vegas odds on its long-term survival. Honestly, this book does not contain enough vigor to warrant even a bad review, yet if I am to write of it I feel more trees shouldn't be sacrificed to a soulless cash-grab when there are so many wonderful works exploring similar territory. Buy any one of the books cited above before purchasing *Horror Culture.* All will cost significantly less while rewarding you multiple times over this absence of effort.

Marvelous Monsters

Hank Wagner

ANYA MARTIN. *Sleeping with the Monster*. Amherst, MA: Lethe Press, 2018. 280 pp. $19.00 tpb. ISBN: 978-1-59021-700-9.

Loyal canines feature prominently in two of the twelve stories (ten short tales, plus two novellas) featured in this slim, entertaining volume. Its opening tale, "A Girl and Her Dog," demonstrates how far we go to protect those we love. "Old Tsah-hov," reminiscent of Jack London's *The Call of the Wild,* tells the life story of a wild animal, tamed by its love for its master.

Less loyal (and less savory) are many of the men who are featured in the lives of Martin's heroines. There's "Window," where a lost love holds sway over a woman's current love interest; "Passage to the Dreamtime," which proves in a ghastly way that the heart wants what the heart wants; "Prince of Lyghes," whose strange dénouement gives new meaning to the term "all consuming love"; and two novellas, "Jehessimen," wherein the heroine discovers a decidedly strange heritage, and "Grass," which reminded this reader of Alan Moore's classic run in *Swamp Thing*. In each, the bad (male) actor meets an appropriate, albeit grisly demise.

Martin shines when she's simply trying to scare us, as in "Resonator Superstar!," which reveals the dark secret behind an odd work of art, or "The Unbride," a Kim Newman-esque takeoff on the classic film *The Bride of Frankenstein,* featuring the actress Elsa Lanchester and the brain of Eleanor Marx. There is also "Boisea triviatta," a tale of an infestation that called to mind Stephen King's "They're Creeping Up on You"; "Sensoria," a sordid saga of sex, drugs, and rock 'n' roll, which captures the often transcendent experience of concert going; and "Black Stone Roses," a dark, strangely romantic vignette in which a Parisian gargoyle comes to life to take a life.

Martin is a skilled, passionate writer, always taking her attention-grabbing premises to their outer limits. Although she wears her influences on her sleeve, she manages to give her stories their own surprising twists. As her title suggests, she often confronts the subject of love, its nature, its value, and, unfortunately, the many ways it can be perverted. These wide-ranging, often unsettling stories establish her as an author with an original, distinct point of view, elegantly expressed, someone worth following as she periodically reports in via her fiction to express her unique perspective on the human condition.

Men Kill Women Like Me

Fiona Maeve Geist

FARAH ROSE SMITH. *Anonyma*. Warren, RI: Ulthar Press. 2019. 121 pp. $17.95 tpb. ISBN: 978-0-359-23948-1.

> "He hated me for this resistance. I aged beyond the confines of clocks and bodies. . . . Men write songs about girls like me, and then they kill them. I still think of him that way—his songs were ice-in-photographs. I still should have been the girl who lived in the way of everything, jumping around corners and speaking *far too* loudly—to awaken, to rise. A girl made woman in a cage."
>
> —Farah Rose Smith, *Anonyma*

The prologue to *Anonyma* opens with an extended meditation on the events that shape the novella, a prolonged coming to terms with abuse and the act of naming it as such—even if the word that prominently shapes contemporary discourse is an elusive phantasm within the text itself. The narrator elides over directly describing events and naming her experiences as cultic, but rather works through a jumble of images in "this moment of boredom to replace shame." There is a tension established at the onset between ambivalence about violence and naming violence and lingering questions about muses and inspiration—one that is immediately troubled by the interview of Nicholas Georg Bezalel in the first chapter of the book. This conversation even contains his disquieting statement that he no longer ascribes "to the practice of having *muses,* per se, as I have found it often to be too exploitative, too direct." This statement is followed by a committed refusal to speak about his (maligned by feminists) photographic exhibition—the titular Anonyma from which the narrator derives her sobriquet; which he brushes aside with an appeal to separate artist from art, claiming that the project was misunderstood. The remainder of the text is an extended reflection on the silence in the conversation—concerning mystical works of Goethern El-

82 Dead Reckonings

lis Von Aurovitch, and their study by Anonyma and Bezalel. However, the text is not an attempt to peel back the curtain on the *idea* that behind every great man there is (perhaps) a tormented woman—akin to the voyeurist sensationalism that Hitchcock (another man whose legacy is troubled by his treatment of his muses) described how blondes "make the best victims. They're like virgin snow that shows up the bloody footprints." Rather, the text concerns itself with the experience of being a muse, a sort of constant psychic degradation and terror interspersed with acts of violence. Yet *Anonyma* refuses to assign passivity to the narrator; she is neither a mute subject nor one who simply acquiesced.

There is a certain element of resistance always present in the experiences that Anonyma undergoes, as Bezalel, in his idolization of Von Aurovitch, claims that she cannot be a true fan:

> for I cannot name every brush stroke, every sculpted mass, every creature! I cannot recite the passages in the adapted tongue. I cannot even hypothesize as to the inner thoughts of the blue lady. This I tell him, so that I can let my ribs heal from the last. I know her through her eyes, even without the original to examine . . . her pain, her suffering—might Von Aurovitch have been such a horrid man as that?

What Anonyma undergoes provokes terse questions about violence. That is, the text, provocatively, continually seems to be asking if artists ever truly understand their muse or if the muse is simply someone tortured by narcissistic artists when bested by their own inadequacy to the task. The lingering argument throughout the text is that Bezalel may have missed the point of their study entirely and that only Anonyma truly understands the work they both value. Bleeding into this are the cycles of violence entangled with the production of art, woven throughout a text rapidly alternating between being chilling and beautiful.

This is a fairly robust description about what the book is 'about' but has very little to say about what actually occurs—and that is a tension throughout Farah Rose Smith's work. There is a hazy, dreamlike quality to the recollections spooling through the text, tangling, snarling, and refusing a simple and tidy summary. There is a constant mobility to the focus, with events occurring out of order or in ambiguous order along with a bleedover between Smith's recurrent "Land of Other," a mythical space for which no explanation is ever fully proffered and yet which seems potent and awash in symbolic and thematic linkages; yet how 'real' these experiences are and how they connect the creative act to mystical initiation. What passes through the reader is a beguiling and baroque world suffused with meaning and saturated with symbols yet left for the reader interrogate how the jagged pieces fit together, as the opacity of the temporal/chronological flow of images demands a fairly significant engagement with the text as a challenging yet elegant and stylish puzzle to be approached— startlingly rich with the elliptical pauses that are more common to short fiction in which the dark and mysterious are never adequately explained and yet remain a lurking dark.

The challenge of assailing the text is rewarding and well worth the price of admission, as disturbing as the contents may be. There is something refreshing about the direct challenges interspersed in the text confronting readers with the question of what they are reading. For example, when Anonyma directly addresses the common dismissals of abuse by great men, castigating those who

> seek to blame me for my burden. Who see the bruises on my face and believe I deserve them. They have to believe that. How else could they reconcile such a thing, before them? If I were innocent, and marked, then an injustice has been done. An injustice has been laid out before them. And one is meant to act in the face of injustice, not walk away. Cowardice lives in that walking. So they believe that I am deserving of this mark. Of this horrid life of mine. To think it could happen to them, or their innocent children. That this is the way of evil. And you turn from it every day, not wanting any involvement.

In this confrontation, and the dazzling style employed by Smith throughout, *Anonyma* joins the growing ranks of contemporary weird stories (such as those of Priya Sharma, Selena Chambers, and Sunny Moraine) that delve into a deeply uncomfortable space where the fantastical seeps into the mundanity of quotidian violence, a dark mirror interrogating reality. A text this difficult and rewarding (both in terms of content and style) is a precious thing that highlights what is most vital and worthwhile in literary exploration.

Meditations on the Agnostic Gothic

Karen Joan Kohoutek

"What can produce a greater terror than the idea of an angry god?"—John Dennis, *The Grounds of Criticism in Poetry*

"To an atheist, the sacraments are as silly as a séance."—Wendy Kaminer, *Sleeping with Extra-terrestrials: The Rise of Irrationalism and Perils of Piety*

When the Gothic genre was developed in the eighteenth and nineteenth centuries, tales of horror and the supernatural were embedded in a cultural environment that assumed an orderly Christian universe. The very word "Gothic" arises from its use in church architecture, repurposed to evoke a romantic medieval past, but its use didn't necessarily evoke a simplistic view of otherworldly matters. Horace Walpole tagged his pioneering work *The Castle of Otranto* (1764) as "a Gothic tale," popularizing the use of the term to describe the supernatural and macabre, but while he believed that "a Gothic church or a convent fills one with romantic dreams," he also thought that, as far as "the Church in the abstract" was concerned, "it is a jargon that means nothing . . . and I reject it and its apostles" (191).

Various scholars have taken different points of view on the relationship of the supernatural to more or less conventional spiritual beliefs. E. J. Clery describes a period, particularly related to the "explained supernatural" in the works of Ann Radcliffe, when "the lessons of Providence found an ideal vehicle in Gothic fictions where invisible agency constitutes a key mystery to be resolved." She asserts that the frequent "bizarre coincidences" of romance function as "evidence of a higher supernaturalism that ensures every 'accident' has its rightful place in the schema of Divine Justice" (*The Rise of Supernatural Fiction* 112).

Similarly, in discussing Samuel Johnson's interest in the 1762 Cock Lane ghost sighting, she relates how his biographer James Boswell "attempted to make clear the nature of Johnson's commitment to the supernatural. Its source was doubt: an extreme horror of death which made proof of the immortality of souls an urgent necessity" (18). The popularity of supernatural fiction is likened to the interest in this supposedly "real" haunting, forms of a trend that "emerges out of the ideological division between believers and skeptics which characterizes the problematic of the 'real' supernatural" (17). As the truth cannot truly be known, only believed, the belief in supernatural beings directly mirrors the belief in a Christian God, ultimately more a matter of faith rather than logical proof.

In complete contrast, Richard Davenport-Hines casually brushed off the importance of religious belief in Gothic works, suggesting that the weakening of religious belief in the eighteenth and nineteenth centuries actually strengthened the development of the Gothic. "As credence in the devil and hell have receded along with Christianity, people have played at being the devil or have devised new forms of hell" (1).

The experience of the spiritual and supernatural in the twentieth and twenty-first centuries is even more complex, being more fragmented, encompassing a spectrum with many varieties of belief and disbelief, and a tendency toward agnosticism: "one who holds that the existence of anything beyond and behind material phenomena is unknown and (so far as can be judged) unknowable" (*Oxford English Dictionary* 260). An agnostic strain, interacting with spiritual uncertainty, runs throughout the history of the Gothic, its presence sometimes growing more prominent, sometimes becoming a theme in its own right.

Countless works could have been used to illustrate these ideas, but a few have been chosen to represent forms of Gothic fiction that recognize spiritual complexities and lean toward agnostic questions.

John Dennis, whose work in the early eighteenth century predated the Gothic genre, is described as "innovative . . . in arguing the connection between the sublime and the emotion of terror" (Clery and Miles 101), an idea later developed by the better-known philosopher Edmund Burke. "Nothing,"

Dennis states, "is so terrifying as the wrath of Infinite Power, because nothing is so unavoidable as the vengeance designed by it. There is no flying nor lying hid from the great universal Monarch. He may deliver us from other terrors, but nothing can save and defend us from Him" (103).

Matthew Gregory Lewis's influential 1794 novel *The Monk* vividly describes similar concerns. When the villain Ambrosio faces death, he realizes the enormity of his sins. "In this Labyrinth of terrors, fain would He have taken his refuge in the gloom of Atheism," but "he could not help feeling the existence of a God. Those truths, once his comfort, now presented themselves before him in the clearest light" (425). Without even the certainty of atheism for comfort, that light is the true source of his horror.

This is a very different perspective from that of most modern readers, who are less likely to assume the existence of any dominant religious philosophy. Even the struggles in a popular work like *Dracula* may be difficult for many to relate to. As scholar Elizabeth Miller says, "A case can be made that *Dracula* is a reaffirmation of Christian teachings in the face of nineteenth century skepticism." She adds that "this reading may be outdated" (205), but the novel itself emphasizes the importance of the eternal soul, a major concern completely ignored in the many modern film adaptations.

For example, the undead Lucy needs be tracked down and staked in part because "when this now Un-Dead be made to rest as true dead, then the soul of the poor lady . . . shall again be free" (215). There are numerous other quotes on the same theme, as when Mina, herself infected by the vampire's attack, calls herself "a poor weak woman, whose soul perhaps is lost" (330).

This religious perspective is in some way based on a belief in the reality of something unseen, however that something is described. Part of the imaginative linkage between the spiritual and the supernatural may lie in the nature of how people perceive and accept those parts of reality that are intangible and non-concrete. The way in which they experience the unseen, and whatever is not definitively, unambiguously knowable, informs their relationships with the religious/spiritual, the supernatural (that which is either explained or accepted at face value), and even knowledge itself. Our thoughts are as unseen as the heaven that some people believe awaits us after death or the ghosts that some believe walk among us. Much of life is not on the surface, and everyday life, with its currents of coincidence and imagination, can contain more mystery than is often recognized.

Wherever the limits between them are drawn, the forms of the spiritual, the superstitious, and the supernatural all involve the unseen, and, although they may still hold out the hope of analysis and eventual understanding, the potentially unknowable.

Frequently, the spiritual and the supernatural are confused, or at least intermingled, in the general consciousness, and this was certain common in late eighteenth and early nineteenth centuries, when the word "superstition," something a rational thinker in our time is expected to move beyond, was common used to describe Christian belief. Ann Radcliffe's *The Italian* (1797), for example, describes a convent's religious decorations as "roughly painted with subjects indicatory of the severe superstitions of the place" (66). When the novel's hero Vivaldi and villain Schedoni confront each other, the latter claims to have taken advantage of the former's "prevailing weakness . . . a susceptibility which renders you especially liable to superstition," at which Vivaldi exclaims, "What! does a monk call superstition a weakness?" (397).

The linkage of the spiritual and the supernatural is reminiscent of Patricia Meyer Spacks's description of the shifts in religious philosophies in the eighteenth century; for example, quoting John Wesley that "giving up witchcraft is, in effect, giving up the Bible" (20). It seems logical that, as the belief of people in the traditionally spiritual would wane, their belief in the larger supernatural would as well. But neither the religious impulse nor the attraction to the supernatural has fully gone away. We still see a range of belief that dualists can divide into more or less positive extremes: for example, piety and faith versus mere superstition, openmindedness versus gullibility, intellectual curiosity and a search for truth versus a rejection of faith in order to clear the way to do evil.

In *Ann Radcliffe: The Great Enchantress,* Robert Miles suggests that "superstition, a mental weakness traditionally reviled as the chief instrument of Catholic obscurantism and oppression" became popular, even "fashionable" in largely Protestant Britain, by virtue of the time's "decay in traditional theological structures" (13). He claims that even the popular "upsurge in religious feeling" created a "very multiplicity of socially licit beliefs [that] served to underline the absence of any authoritative base" (14). Despite the great differences between Ann Radcliffe's time and ours, this "absence of any authoritative base" has a ring of familiarity. The anti-Catholic tendencies of *The Italian* have often been discussed, for example by Robert Miles, but the faith of other characters, even as it is specifically Catholic, is treated respectfully by Radcliffe. The different convents seen in *The Italian,* for example, operate more as social microcosms than vehicles for propaganda. Although the heroine Ellena suffers under the "supercilious haughtiness" of the Abbess of San Stefano (67), the convent where she is imprisoned, she also meets the saintly Olivia, who is both pious and kind, in the same place. In addition, San Stefano is contrasted to the earlier-seen convent, to which Ellena and her aunt had been "for some years amicably connected" (47).

Thus, while corruption is seen to exist within religious institutions, there is also a sincerity of faith—both darkness and light—just as there is in the larger world outside. Religion may be either a disguise for evil or a consolation for its existence. This framework is part of the reason why Radcliffe's work is associated with a conventional mainstream morality, even as it depicts the problematic nature of blind trust in religion and religious authorities.

Similar situations will reappear in James Hogg's *Confessions of a Justified Sinner* (1824), in the context of a completely different religious system. This work explores not only the erosion of religious certainty, but depicts how that previous certainty created the horrific elements, with the knowledge that this faith may have been misplaced.

In this novel, the religious authority is a Calvinist who believes the "elect" are preordained by God. He leads another character, the titular sinner, Robert Wringhim, into committing evil acts, persuading him that a specific murder is "the duty of one consecrated to God" (113). Wringhim's reaction is that "I approved of it in theory, but my spirit stood aloof from the practice . . . it was only at the earnest and unceasing instigations of my enlightened and voluntary patron that I at length put my hand to the conclusive work" (114).

Everything Wringhim does is intended to be in the service of heaven, yet he clearly develops doubts about his final destination, and whether or not he believes in the correct cosmology. When he thinks of his victims being sentenced to Hell, he contemplates: "Will there not be a sentence pronounced against me there, by a jury of the just made perfect, and written down in the registers of Heaven?" (133). Eventually, the friend he once believed "bent on establishing some pure and genuine doctrines of Christianity" becomes one he "now dreaded more than Hell" (152, 156).

Wringhim's problem is reminiscent of the circular reasoning inherent in the appeal to the Bible as the source of truth, as in the childhood song, "Jesus loves me, this I know / For the Bible tells me so." How do we know the Bible reveals the real truth and the word of God? Because the Bible says so. But who has the right to start claiming divine revelation? Hogg's protagonist gets in a bind because he vacillates on the question of how he can *know* what God wants, how he can know the real spiritual truth. He believes he is among the elect, and believes he is performing the will of God, but he cannot be absolutely, positively certain of the source of his information and its reliability. Under these circumstances, he cannot know, as a fact, what God really wants from him.

The situation in this novel is highly exaggerated, but at its thematic heart is a question that plagues Christianity: we don't know, we can only believe. The human religious experience, at least as it involves the traditional Judeo-Christian God figure, cannot be direct, but instead is mediated by the structures of a specific religious system. This forces individuals to believe in something on faith alone, with no concrete evidence to guide them. Even mystics, who may believe they have some direct evidence of the "truth," only have the conviction of their own personal perception. In this morass, there is only interpretation, with the immortal soul at stake.

When different, equally reputable religious figures and thinkers disagree, how do we know whom to believe? If all our knowledge of God must be mediated, who is entrusted to do the mediating, with our souls supposedly hanging in the balance? For Wringhim, depending on how trustworthy his sources are, he is either going to a heavenly reward or to eternal torment, with no possibility of an in-between. In the end, he makes some proto-existential statements applicable to the position of almost anyone on earth: "I was a being incomprehensible to myself," and "Thus was I sojourning in the midst of a chaos of confusion" (151, 152).

In some Gothic works, the supernatural blends with the natural, leaving ambiguous what part is played by the perceived God, as in J. Sheridan Le Fanu's "Green Tea" (1872). Here, a Christian vicar, the Rev. Mr. Jennings, is plagued by seemingly supernatural visions of an evil monkey, which eventually hounds him to his death. In addition to his apparently conventional Christian faith, he has been studying the work of Swedish mystic Emanuel Swedenborg (8–9), an interest he shares with the narrator, Dr. Hesselius, who draws from it the philosophy that "the entire natural world is but the ultimate expression of that spiritual world from which, and in which alone, it has its life" (4).

In this story, the monkey itself is never explained by the author, so we never know if it is hallucination or a "supernatural" manifestation, one that might expose something strange about the natural order, given the Swedenborgian idea that the natural is, in essence, a reflection of the spiritual. That possibility is muddied by the fact that Dr. Hesselius himself, despite his high-sounding professed ideas about spiritual causes, attributes the appearance of the monkey to an imbalance created by "the habitual use of such agents as green tea" (29).

This diagnosis not only seems entirely unsatisfactory for a persecuting vision that will drive a decent man to suicide, but it also seems disappointingly material and prosaic. The paradigm in which material things contain spiritual meanings is inverted, so that the potentially spiritual, or at least supernatural, is explained away as having a simple, even trivial, material cause.

A work such as "Green Tea" illustrates the position of human beings in a world where, even if a belief in a Christian God is true, the actions and motives of that being are truly ineffable and unknowable, which leads to a situation of horror. This is one of the ways that Le Fanu's works seem particularly modern, even looking forward to existentialism. They are "unfettered by an orderly moral universe," taking place instead in "a uniquely hostile cosmos" (Sullivan 129, 125). His characters often cannot be certain about their position relative to an unseen God, or readily believe that this God provides an orderly structure and meaning to the universe even if it cannot be understood. "Various characters suggest various possibilities—all of them bleak—yet final solutions elude them, as they elude the reader" (ibid).

The long tradition of conflating the spiritual and the supernatural perhaps explains why religious iconography still gives a kick to artistic representations of horror, even in a time when many people no longer believe with the literalness they once did. In an era without an assumption of unified religious belief, instead encompassing a vast variety of individual experiences and spiritual subcultures, religious questions and supernatural tales lie equally in the realm of the uncertain and unknowable. While a mass audience may no longer readily relate to the fear of an angry God, uncertainty about the larger spiritual concerns has always had its uncanny side, to which the Gothic has always appealed.

Works Cited

Clery, E. J. *The Rise of Supernatural Fiction: 1762–1800*. Cambridge: Cambridge University Press, 1995.

———, and Robert Miles, ed. *Gothic Documents: A Sourcebook 1700–1820*. Manchester: Manchester University Press, 2000.

Davenport-Hines, Richard. *Gothic: Four Hundred Years of Excess, Horror, Evil and Ruin*. New York: Farrar, Straus & Giroux., 1998.

Hogg, James. *Confessions of a Justified Sinner*. 1824. New York: Alfred A. Knopf, 1992.

Le Fanu, J. Sheridan. "Green Tea." In *Green Tea and Other Ghost Stories*. New York: Dover, 1993.

Lewis, Matthew Gregory. *The Monk*. 1794. Oxford: Oxford University Press, 1973

Miles, Robert. *Ann Radcliffe: The Great Enchantress*. Manchester: Manchester University Press, 1995.

Miller, Elizabeth. *Reflections on* Dracula: *Ten Essays*. White Rock, BC: Transylvania Press, 1997.

Oxford English Dictionary. 2nd edition. Prepared by J. A. Simpson and E. S. C. Weiner. Oxford: Clarendon Press, 1989.

Radcliffe, Ann. *The Italian; or, The Confessional of the Black Penitents: A Romance*. 1797. Oxford: Oxford University Press, 1998.

Spacks, Patricia Meyer. *The Insistence of Horror: Aspects of the Supernatural in Eighteenth-Century Poetry*. Cambridge, MA: Harvard University Press, 1962.

Stoker, Bram. *Dracula*. 1897. Oxford: Oxford University Press, 1983.

Sullivan, Jack. "'Green Tea': The Archetypal Ghost Story." In *Literature of the Occult: A Collection of Critical Essays,* ed. Peter B. Messent. Englewood Cliffs, NJ: Prentice-Hall, 1981.

Walpole, Horace. *The Letters of Horace Walpole, Earl of Orford: Including Numerous Letters Now First Published from the Original Manuscripts*. Vol. 4. Philadelphia: Lea & Blanchard, 1842.

About the Contributors

Michael J. Abolafia is an editor, writer, archivist with a B.A. in English from Columbia University, and co-editor of *Dead Reckonings*.

David Barker's latest books are *Witches in Dreamland* (2018), a Lovecraftian novel written with W. H. Pugmire, and *Half in Light, Half in Shadow* (2019), a chapbook of weird fiction.

Ramsey Campbell is an English horror fiction writer, editor, and critic who has been writing for well over fifty years. He is frequently cited as one of the leading writers in the field. His website is www.ramseycampbell.com.

Fiona Maeve Geist lives with her cat in WXXT country, where she freelances RPGs and writes short fiction. Her work has appeared in *Lamplight Quarterly,* CLASH Media, *Mothership* (RPG), and *Ashes and Entropy* (forthcoming).

Edward Guimont is a Ph.D. candidate at the University of Connecticut Department of History.

Alex Houstoun is a co-editor of *Dead Reckonings*.

S. T. Joshi is the author of such critical studies as *The Weird Tale* (1990), *H. P. Lovecraft: The Decline of the West* (1990), and *Unutterable Horror: A History of Supernatural Fiction* (2012). He has prepared corrected editions of H. P. Lovecraft's work for Arkham House and annotated editions of the weird tales of Lovecraft, Algernon Blackwood, Lord Dunsany, M. R. James, Arthur Machen, and Clark Ashton Smith for Penguin Classics, as well as the anthology *American Supernatural Tales* (2007).

Karen Joan Kohoutek, an independent scholar and poet, has published about weird fiction in various journals and literary websites. Recent and upcoming publications have been on subjects including the Gamera films, the Robert E. Howard/H. P. Lovecraft correspondence, folk magic in the novels of Ishmael Reed, and the proto-Gothic writer Charles Brockden Brown. She lives in Fargo, North Dakota.

Michael D. Miller is an adjunct professor and NEH medievalist summer scholar with numerous one-act play productions, awards, and optioned screenplays to his credit, and is the author of the *Realms of Fantasy RPG* for Mythopoeia Games Publications. His poetry has appeared *Spectral Realms* and scholarly publications in *Lovecraft Annual*.

Danel Olson is the conceiver and contributing editor of a six-volume original fiction print series, *Exotic Gothic* (Ash-Tree Press, PS Publishing). His other edited works include *21st Century Gothic: Great Gothic Fiction Since 2000* (Scarecrow Press) and *The Exorcist, Stanley Kubrick's The Shining,* and *Guillermo del Toro's The Devil's Backbone and Pan's Labyrinth,* all in Centipede Press's Studies in the Horror Film series (the latter two were finalists for the Bram Stoker Award).

Daniel Pietersen is a writer of weird fiction and horror philosophy. He has a blog of fragmentary work and other thoughts at https://constantuniversity.wordpress.com.

Géza A. G. Reilly is a writer and critic with an interest in twentieth-century American genre literature. A Canadian expatriate, he now lives in the wilds of Florida with his wife, Andrea, and their cat, Mim.

Christopher Ropes is an author and musician who lives in New Jersey with his partner, their two children, and their cats. His work has been published by Dunhams Manor/Dynatox Industries and *Vastarien: A Literary Journal*.

Darrell Schweitzer is an American writer, editor, and critic in the field of speculative fiction. Much of his focus has been on dark fantasy and horror, although he does also work in science fiction and fantasy. His latest book *The Dragon House*.

Bev Vincent is the author of several books. His work has been nominated for the Bram Stoker Award (twice), the Edgar Award, and the ITW Thriller Award, and he won the 2010 Al Blanchard Award. His reviews also appear at *Onyx Reviews* (onyxreviews.com). He is a contributing editor with *Cemetery Dance* and has published more than eighty short stories. His web presence is bevvincent.com.

Hank Wagner is a respected critic and journalist. Among the many publications in which his work regularly appears are *Cemetery Dance* and *Mystery Scene*.